Using the Standards

Teacher Resource

Grade Five

Published by Instructional Fair • TS Denison
an imprint of

McGraw Hill Children's Publishing

Editor: Rebecca Warren
Teacher Consultant: Becky Daniel

Children's Publishing

Published by Instructional Fair • TS Denison
An imprint of McGraw-Hill Children's Publishing

Send all inquiries to:
McGraw-Hill Children's Publishing
3195 Wilson Drive NW
Grand Rapids, Michigan 49544

Using the Standards: Teacher Resource—grade 5
ISBN: 0-7424-1945-2

1 2 3 4 5 6 7 8 9 PHXBK 09 08 07 06 05 04
The McGraw-Hill Companies

Table of Contents

Reading

Language Arts

Math

Science

Social Studies

Introduction

You can hardly spend a day in the world of education without hearing about standards. Teachers are asked to incorporate an increasingly complex array of state standards into an already crowded curriculum. But how do theoretical concepts translate into real-life student work? *Using the Standards* will help you fill your classroom with solid standards-based activities and answer your most pressing questions:

- How do I know what standards to follow?
- What grade-appropriate activities can I use with my students?
- How can I perform accurate and specific assessment for my students?
- What is the best way to prepare my students for standardized tests?

Developed with tested ideas from experienced teachers, this book is filled with ideas for making your classroom a dynamic, content-rich environment.

Finding "Your" Standards

Which standards should you follow? If your school has not specified which standards you are to follow, or if you are a home-based educator, a good place to start is your state standards. Most state standards can be found on the state's official web page under "education" (**www.statename.gov**).

Hot Tip

State Standards the Easy Way. There is an easier way! Align to Achieve, Inc. has done the work for you. This not-for-profit organization has compiled state standards for every state into one easy-to-search database. You can find this database at: **www.aligntoachieve.org**.

National Standards?

Implementing standards-based education is not dependent on state models, however. Many agencies have issued so-called "national" standards. While an agreed-upon set of national standards does not, in fact, exist, there are nonetheless common themes throughout the different standard articulations. National standards are referenced in this book for each subject area only to provide a starting point for exploration into your own state or district standards. This book has been designed to cover a broad range of topics addressed by most standards. Give your students a solid foundation by working through the basic skills in this book, and you will find that every student can be far more than "up to standard."

How to Use This Book

Correlation to Standards

Begin with the "Correlation to Standards" chart on pages 10–12. After you have found your state standards (see page 4 for hints on how to do this), check the information for each content area to see which pages cover certain skills. Blank spaces are available in the chart for you to record correlations to your own set of standards.

Parent Letter

As you begin to incorporate standards into your classroom, you may want to communicate this to parents. Use the "Parent Letter" on page 9 to let parents know what you are doing in the classroom and why. While most parents are aware that their children are required to take certain standardized tests, they often do not know that these tests are based on standards. The more involved the parents are in supporting your effort to include standards in the curriculum, the more likely your students will succeed.

Content Areas

See the individual content areas for more information about how to find standards-based material for that subject. Each subject area has its own distinctive icon to help you locate material quickly. This book contains the following content areas:

Reading

Language Arts

Math

Science

Social Studies

For each of these content areas, an information page explains the key features of standards in that subject. A clear summary of typical skills required by most standards for that area is followed by a list of classroom activities.

Activity Lists

You know the standards—now what? To help you translate theory into practice, we include an activity list for each subject area. Developed by experienced teachers who have used these activities in their classrooms, this list provides a great starting place for implementing the standards in your classroom. A variety of activities are included to appeal to different learning styles.

How to Use This Book

Sample Tests

Sample tests are included for each subject area. The tests are designed to give your students practice with the types of questions they may be asked on standardized tests. Use sample tests before beginning a new content area to identify skills that students need to practice, or use them after working through the activity pages to assess progress. See "Assessment Tips" on pages 7–8 for more ideas on measuring student achievement.

Skill Pages

Each content area includes skill-specific reproducible pages to use with your students. The pages included are not comprehensive, but do cover a broad range of expectations within each content area. Make as many copies as you need for your class and distribute to students. The skill pages can be done individually or in groups, in class as part of a center or at home. You may want to combine skill pages with ideas in the "Activity List" for each subject to help you develop your daily lesson plans.

Critical Thinking Themes

Look for the following themes on each page to help your students develop cross-curricular critical thinking skills:

- Explore
- Discover
- Organize
- Communicate
- Summarize

As students begin to explore the content of their world, discover new things, organize their thinking, communicate to others, and clearly summarize what they have learned, they will grow in their ability to analyze new information.

The value of standards-based learning is not simply to reach an end—performance on state tests, but for a beginning—allowing students to be full participants and investigators of the world around them.

Assessment Tips

All Students Can Succeed

One of the fundamental beliefs of a standards-based model for education is that all students can succeed. Rather than start with the assumption that a class will naturally include some students who will not succeed, teachers should start with the premise that all students can (and will) meet the standard. Students may differ in the ways they get there, but each should expect to achieve the same end result. The usefulness of the standards-based model is that it clearly and specifically states what that end result is to be. The challenge is to decide how to encourage learning that allows students at a wide range of skill levels to meet the standards and how to appropriately assess them along the way.

Assessment Requires Parent Involvement

Get parents involved early and often in the education of their child. Use the letter provided on page 9 to inform parents about the standards you will be covering and the tests (if any) that their child will be required to take. It is important to communicate to parents that one day of testing is nurtured by many days of involvement. Do what you can to keep parents up-to-date on the areas their child struggles with to encourage extra practice at home. As parents ask questions, review homework, and stay informed about learning goals, they will provide a sound platform for student success on standardized tests.

Assessment Is Ongoing

Whether aware of it or not, every teacher performs continuous assessment of students during class. How many times have you answered these questions during a class period?

- Which students offer answers quickly?
- Which students need more time to work through a problem?
- Who needs to use a hands-on tool to understand something?
- Who needs quiet time alone to work through a problem?
- Are there students who look frustrated? What do they need to help them understand?
- How can I adapt this lesson to encourage understanding?

Teachers naturally consider each student's progress as they move through a lesson. While it may be impossible to tailor learning for each member of a class, teachers should provide multiple opportunities for students to succeed. A variety of tools for solving problems will help students with different learning styles to grasp essential concepts. This may include use of pictures, models, or other hands-on materials.

Instead of putting all the focus on the day of "the big test," create portfolios of student work throughout a unit. These can show progress in student thinking on a topic from the early days of learning to the end. They can also provide a flag for potential problem areas before testing occurs.

Assessment Tips

Assessment Is Varied

When designing tests, use a variety of formats. Depending on the age of your students, any of the following may be appropriate question types:

- true and false
- multiple choice
- matching
- fill-in-the-blank
- graphic organizers
- open-ended or essay

With younger students, you could also use one-on-one interviews to ask questions out loud and listen to students explain their answers.

Using a variety of types of assessment will allow students many different ways to show what they know. Encourage students to show the process they used to figure out an answer. Even if they did not achieve the correct end result, they may have a solid grasp of concepts. Showing all their work will identify the specific place their solution process went awry.

Hot Tip

Begin with the End in Mind. Have you ever made it to the end of a great lesson series and found yourself stuck for ways to measure student progress? Rather than thinking of assessment as the end result, try beginning with the end in mind.

As you plan a new lesson series, consider what objectives you would like students to meet. Then ask yourself, how will I know if students have met those objectives? As you map out daily lesson plans, consider how each lesson will give students another tool to succeed on the testing they will face at the end of the unit.

Test Practice

For complete practice in all content areas, see the McGraw-Hill Children's Publishing *Spectrum Test Practice* series. With a book for each grade level, this series provides a variety of practice questions and sample tests addressing the same standards used in this book.

Promoting the
Standards
•encourage•remind•create•review•praise

Dear Parent/Guardian:

We have begun using activities in our classroom that are based on educational standards. "Standards" are guidelines for skills that students should know in a particular grade. Often standardized tests measure student achievement in these standard skills. By focusing our classroom activities on the standards, we are allowing the students to have as much practice as possible in these basic skills.

You can support your child's learning by understanding the standards that are required for his/her grade level. The standards that we are following can be found at

____.

Your child will/will not be tested this year. The state test your child will take will be on ____________________________. I am available at any time to review testing results and discuss how these scores affect your child's progress.

Encourage your child to rest well and eat a good breakfast before the test. You can help your child develop testing confidence by being involved in their learning throughout the school year.

To help your child do his/her best with this material, follow these guidelines:

- Encourage your child to be curious about the world.
- Remind your child to ask questions about things he/she does not understand in class.
- Create time for your child to share what he/she has discovered at school.
- Review the skill pages your child brings home. Ask which things your child had difficulty understanding.
- Praise your child often for learning. The end results on a single day of testing cannot measure enthusiasm, curiosity, or the joy of discovery.

With parents and teachers partnering together, we can be sure that our children are far more than "up to standard"!

Sincerely,

Correlation to Standards

Grade 5

Sample Standards	Using the Standards Grade 5	*CAT Level for Gr. 5	**CTBS Level for Gr. 5	Other
Reading				
Vocabulary				
Using synonyms	17, 21, 22, 31	x	x	
Using antonyms	17, 21		x	
Using homophones	20			
Using multi-meaning words	20		x	
Using common roots and word parts				
Comprehension				
Identifying main idea	19	x	x	
Identifying supporting details	23, 30, 35	x	x	
Identifying sequence of events		x	x	
Drawing conclusions (inferencing)	19, 27, 31	x	x	
Comparing and contrasting	23, 25	x	x	
Identifying cause and effect	36	x	x	
Identifying character traits/feelings	20, 34, 35	x	x	
Distinguishing between fact and opinion	19, 33	x		
Using graphic organizers	25	x	x	
Summarizing	29, 30, 31	x	x	
Identifying author's purpose		x	x	
Reading various genres	28, 29	x	x	
Understanding theme	38			
Language Arts				
Mechanics and Expression				
Using correct capitalization and punctuation	42, 55	x	x	
Determining correct usage	43, 53, 55	x	x	
Recognizing complete sentences	52	x	x	
Using simple and compound sentences	45, 51, 53	x		
Identifying topic sentences for paragraphs	44, 49	x	x	
Identifying supporting sentences for paragraphs	50	x	x	
Using different types of writing	43, 48			
Identifying correct and incorrect spelling	45, 56		x	

*Terra Nova CAT™ ©2001 CTB/McGraw-Hill
**Terra Nova CTBS® ©1997 CTB/McGraw-Hill

Correlation to Standards

Grade 5

Sample Standards	Using the Standards Grade 5	*CAT Level for Gr. 5	**CTBS Level for Gr. 5	Other
Math				
Number and Operations				
Using numbers up to 1,000,000	66	x	x	
Ordering and comparing whole numbers	66, 67, 75, 76	x	x	
Ordering and comparing fractions, decimals, percents	61, 65, 71, 72			
Using integers	68		x	
Understanding place value	65	x	x	
Recognizing fractions and decimals from pictures	61	x	x	
Using operations with fractions, decimals, percents	62, 71, 73, 74	x	x	
Using standard algorithms for operations	69	x	x	
Estimating	72, 74	x	x	
(Pre-)Algebra				
Recognizing patterns	62, 77, 80	x	x	
Using number sentences	62, 78	x	x	
Using symbols to represent numbers	62, 63, 78	x	x	
Geometry				
Using a coordinate grid	81			
Identifying lines, angles, and shapes	84		x	
Identifying parts of a circle	86			
Identifying lines of symmetry	63	x	x	
Identifying congruent figures			x	
Identifying 2-D and 3-D shapes	82, 83		x	
Measurement				
Selecting appropriate units	63, 88			
Finding perimeter and area	63, 85, 89	x		
Using volume				
Adding time intervals	84	x	x	
Making calculations with money	61, 87		x	
Data Analysis and Probability				
Graphing data	64, 94	x	x	
Solving experimental probability situations	64, 90, 91	x	x	
Understanding averages (mean, median, mode)	64, 79, 92, 93		x	
Problem Solving				
Selecting appropriate operations	69, 70, 73, 87	x	x	
Using a variety of methods to solve problems	69, 70, 73, 87	x	x	
Estimating results	72, 74	x	x	
Recognizing reasonable solutions	70	x		

*Terra Nova CAT™ ©2001 CTB/McGraw-Hill
**Terra Nova CTBS® ©1997 CTB/McGraw-Hill

Correlation to Standards

Grade 5

Sample Standards	Using the Standards Grade 5	*CAT Level for Gr. 5	**CTBS Level for Gr. 5	Other
Science				
Science as inquiry	97, 99			
Physical science	98, 100-101			
Life science	97, 102-103	x	x	
Earth and space science	104-105	x	x	
Science and technology	106			
Science in personal and social perspectives	99, 107			
History and nature of science	108			
Social Studies				
Culture				
Time, continuity, and change	111	x	x	
People, places, and environment	114–115	x	x	
Individual development and identity	113, 116–117			
Individuals, groups, and institutions	122			
Power, authority, and governance	122			
Production, distribution, and consumption	112, 118–119, 120	x	x	
Science, technology, and society	111, 121			
Global connections	118-119			
Civic ideals and practices	122			

*Terra Nova CAT™ ©2001 CTB/McGraw-Hill
**Terra Nova CTBS® ©1997 CTB/McGraw-Hill

Standards in Reading

Reading provides the framework on which all other content areas rest. Developing good reading skills will serve students well as they continue to explore ideas in science, mathematics, social studies, and the arts. National initiatives focused on reading point to its importance for future academic and personal achievement. The National Council of Teachers of English (NCTE) standards can be found at: **www.ncte.org/standards**. To be sure your students' reading skills lay the foundation for future success, consider the building blocks of reading: vocabulary and comprehension.

Vocabulary

Vocabulary development begins in the very earliest grades as students learn to recognize words and understand their meanings. As students move on to later grades, their vocabulary grows and their ability to read texts with fluency increases. Standards-based reading activities will give students grade-appropriate practice with the following:

- sight words, compound words, root words
- synonyms, antonyms, homonyms
- multiple-meaning words
- rhyming and rhythmic language
- figurative language

Encourage your students to use a variety of strategies to decode the meaning of unknown words—using a dictionary or thesaurus, using context clues, or looking for common root words. Your students should encounter words in many different ways—from looking at individual words on vocabulary lists, to listening to words read out loud as part of a story. Developing fluency with language means being able to understand words as they are spoken, heard, and written. As students become more adept at working with individual words, they will be able to turn their focus to comprehension and interpretation of what they have read.

Comprehension

Students of all ages should have practice reading a variety of texts, from poetry to stories, from information books to science reports. Create a text-rich classroom by establishing theme-based centers with appropriate reading material. Besides having a small library in the reading corner, why not also include biographies of famous mathematicians along with your math supplies, or history books along with the globes and maps you use for social studies? Students need multiple ways to approach reading, so include a place for listening to stories and a place for writing and responding to what others have written.

Standards in Reading

Hot Tip

Everyone Loves a Story. Students of all ages love stories. To help students develop fluency in reading, plan a regular story time. Go around the room and have students each take a turn reading out loud. This encourages students to develop fluency, listening skills, and comprehension—all while enjoying the what-happens-next excitement that only stories can bring!

Students demonstrate comprehension of what they have read through their ability to identify the following:

- type of writing (genre)
- main idea and supporting details
- sequence of events, cause and effect
- making predictions, drawing conclusions
- author's purpose
- fact and opinion
- character, plot, setting

These skills will vary by grade level, but all have the same purpose—understanding what has been read. A variety of activities can help students focus and interpret what they have read.

- Have your students work with graphic organizers to help them identify key ideas and connections among them.
- Create text-based questions that have students either recollect what they have read or develop strategies for skimming through the text to find an answer.
- Allow your students to create questions of their own or draw a picture in response to what they have read.
- Encourage students to make connections between what they have read and their own life experiences.

As students develop vocabulary and comprehension, they will read with greater fluency and understanding. The foundation set by these basic skills in reading will prove to be strong and solid for the years of learning that are to come.

Activity List

Fifth graders are at the age that they understand irony and sarcasm. They often have a great sense of humor and enjoy jokes, riddles, and parodies. Take advantage of their natural love of humor when teaching reading comprehension. Many of Aesop's fables contain humorous situations that can keep students interested in sharpening comprehension skills (see Activity 1). Students this age are also interested in questioning what they have read, and enjoy opportunities to practice with fact and opinion (see Activity 2). Finally, students need to strengthen vocabulary skills to help them become better readers (see Activity 3).

Activity 1–Aesop–A Great Resource

Standards: Identifying main idea, summarizing, drawing conclusions, identifying character traits/feelings

Goal: Students will use Aesop's fables to sharpen comprehension skills.

Materials: You can find all of Aesop's fables online. Because they are in the public domain, they can be reproduced for the class.

Activity: To set an example of how to use Aesop's fables to teach comprehension skills, *The Dog and the Shadow* is below, along with some sample questions for this activity.

> Once upon a time, a dog was crossing a bridge with a large piece of meat in its mouth. He stopped and looked into the water and saw his own reflection. He mistook his reflection as another dog with a piece of meat in its mouth. *That dog's meat is twice the size of mine*, he thought. In an attempt to attack the other dog and get the larger piece of meat, the dog let go of his meat and jumped into the water. He thus lost both: that which he grasped at in the water, because it was just a reflection, and his own, because the stream swept it away.

1. Write a one-sentence summary of the fable.
2. What life lesson was Aesop trying to teach through this fable?
3. What do you think happened next, after the dog jumped in the water?
4. What do you think the dog thought about on his way home?
5. In a short paragraph, compare this fable to *The Fox and the Grapes*.
6. Write a fable about a different animal that teaches the same concept.
7. Rewrite the fable with a different ending.

Activity List

Activity 2–Fact or Opinion?

Standards: Distinguishing between fact and opinion

Goal: Students will practice distinguishing between fact and opinion by going through a series of statements together.

Materials: A series of statements that are clearly facts or opinions

Activity: Help students practice with fact and opinion by playing "Thumbs Up, Thumbs Down." As the teacher or another student reads a statement, students are to put thumbs up for facts and thumbs down for opinions. Use the examples below or have students create their own statements.

- I think most boys run faster than girls.
- Ants never sleep or play, they only work.
- Doctors have to complete an internship before practicing medicine.
- Eggs taste best when they are fried.
- All the beautiful people eat popcorn.
- A real man drives a Chevy.

Activity 3–In a Pickle

Standards: Using multi-meaning words

Goal: Students will practice using words with multiple meanings by using them in sentences.

Materials: You will need a list of multi-meaning words and paper for each student to write sentences.

Activity: Students are to use the word given in different sentences, one for each meaning, in a random order. They then trade papers and match their classmates' sentences with the appropriate meaning.

Example: pickle

- cucumber that has been preserved in saltwater or vinegar
  (I ate a pickle.)
- difficult or disagreeable situation
  (I'm in a real pickle because I didn't do my homework.)
- to preserve a food in a solution of saltwater or vinegar
  (Mother will pickle the eggs.)

0-7424-1945-2 — *Using the Standards*

Name ______________________ Date ____________

Sample Test

Read each item. Choose the word that means the same or about the same as the underlined word.

1. Complete the assignment.
   - **a.** task
   - **b.** assistant
   - **c.** design
   - **d.** office

2. Focus your attention.
   - **a.** shine
   - **b.** irritate
   - **c.** divide
   - **d.** concentrate

3. Tom waited anxiously for the announcement.
   - **a.** nervously
   - **b.** without concern
   - **c.** quickly
   - **d.** with anger

4. I admire her as a leader.
   - **a.** advise
   - **b.** detest
   - **c.** trust
   - **d.** respect

Read each item. Choose the word that means the opposite of the underlined word.

5. Accept the truth.
   - **a.** deny
   - **b.** understand
   - **c.** illustrate
   - **d.** respect

6. I am very confident of your abilities.
   - **a.** uncertain
   - **b.** assured
   - **c.** proud
   - **d.** neglectful

7. Write a brief description of the project.
   - **a.** important
   - **b.** lengthy
   - **c.** short
   - **d.** casual

8. Those were very generous servings.
   - **a.** large
   - **b.** grateful
   - **c.** small
   - **d.** general

GO

Sample Test (cont.)

Read the passage. Then answer the questions on page 19.

One afternoon in March, I found two silver dollars shining in a half-melted snowbank. *Buried treasure,* was my first thought. So I dug through the snow looking for more. Of course, I just ended up with really cold hands. I slipped the two coins into my pocket and went home colder but richer.

Two days later, Mary Ann and her little sister were searching the snowbanks. *Finders keepers,* was my first thought. I didn't need to get to the *losers weepers* part since Susy was already crying for real.

"I dropped them right here," she said between tears. Her hands were red from digging in the snow.

"Maybe they got shoved down the street by the snowplow. Let's dig over here." Mary Ann's voice sounded optimistic.

They'll never know, was my second thought, and I walked past them toward Wisser's house.

"Phil, have you seen two silver dollars?" asked Mary Ann. Susy looked up from digging. Her eyes were hopeful.

"Coins?" *Look innocent,* was my third thought.

"Yeah, Susy dropped two silver dollars along here last week."

"Silver dollars?"

"Yeah," said Susy. "They're thick and big." She brushed her red hands off on her jacket and wiped the tears from her face. Her eyes were as red as her hands.

Lie, was my fourth thought. "As a matter of fact," I hesitated, "I dug two coins out of that snowbank just a few days ago. I wondered who might have lost them."

Susy leaped on me, hugging me. "Oh, thank you, thank you."

GO

Name ______________________ Date ______________

Sample Test (cont.)

Answer the questions about the story on page 18.

9. What is the main idea of this story?
a. It is okay to lie if you think you will get away with it.
b. It is always better to be honest than rich.
c. "Finders keepers, losers weepers."
d. Both **b** and **c** apply.

10. How did Phil probably feel at the end of the story?
a. angry with himself for being honest
b. angry with Mary Ann and Susy
c. hopeful that he would find another buried treasure
d. disappointed at giving up the coins but glad he was honest

11. What is the problem in the story?
a. Susy has lost two silver dollars in a row.
b. Phil doesn't want to give up the coins he found.
c. Phil doesn't want to help Susy find her coins.
d. Mary Ann doesn't want to help her sister.

12. Which statement below is a fact?
a. Phil thinks only of his own wants.
b. Susy cries too much.
c. Susy and Phil should be wearing mittens out in the snow.
d. Susy is crying because she has lost her silver dollars.

13. What is the setting of this story?
a. outside on a March day
b. outside on a warm, sunny day
c. a cold, winter day
d. the view outside a window

14. What would be a good title for this story?
a. Frostbitten Fingers
b. Finders Keepers, Losers Weepers
c. A Fistful of Dollars
d. Honesty Is Best

GO

Name ______________________ Date ____________

Sample Test (cont.)

Choose the word that correctly completes both sentences.

15. Barb put a clean _______ on the bed.
Jason washed the cookie _______ after baking.

a. pillow
b. tray
c. sheet
d. cover

16. We _______ nearer to the warmth of the campfire.
He _______ the wrong conclusion from the facts that were presented.

a. drew
b. moved
c. identified
d. illustrated

Read the passage below. Then answer the questions.

The birds are chirping. Little green buds are just beginning to form on the branches of the trees. Steven is walking slowly with his head down. He does not notice any of the morning's beauty. He has to decide what to do. His friend Jared wants to skip school today. Steven doesn't want to hurt Jared's feelings, but he knows it is wrong to skip school. Steven looks up and feels a gentle breeze on his face. He sees his school off in the distance. Suddenly, he knows what to do.

17. In what season does the story take place? How do you know?

____

18. Who is the main character?

____

19. What is the character's problem?

____

20. How do you predict the problem will be solved? What details helped you decide this?

____

____

STOP

Name ______________________ Date ______________

Word Play

Words that have similar meanings are called **synonyms**. Words that have opposite meanings are called **antonyms**. Words that sound the same but have different spellings and meanings are called **homophones**.

Look at the following word pairs. Write S next to each pair of synonyms, A next to each pair of antonyms, and H next to each pair of homophones.

1. _______ blue, blew

2. _______ thick, thin

3. _______ plane, plain

4. _______ wrong, incorrect

5. _______ reward, punish

6. _______ amazing, astounding

7. _______ council, counsel

8. _______ giggle, chuckle

Write an antonym and a synonym for each word.

	Antonym	**Synonym**
9. clean	______________	______________
10. connect	______________	______________
11. hilarious	______________	______________
12. generous	______________	______________

Circle the correct homophones to complete the story.

I walked to the county (fair, fare) to buy a (pair, pear) of (hares, hairs). "It (brakes, breaks) my heart to sell them," said the farmer. "As you can see, they are perfectly matched with very soft (fir, fur). They have (one, won) lots of prizes." Finally the farmer agreed to the (sale, sail). I carried the animals all the way into town on that hot day.

I got on the bus to go home. "No animals allowed!" said the driver.

"But these are prize-winning (hairs, hares)!" I protested. "I have a (steak, stake) in getting them home safely. It's (to, two, too) hot a day to walk all the way home with these animals."

The bus driver told me to get off the bus. Fortunately, at that moment I heard the (brakes, breaks) of a truck and a voice yelling, "Hey, (Peat, Pete)!" It was my cousin (Terry, Tarry). Thankfully, he gave me a ride home!

Name ______________________ Date ____________

America's Beauties

Read about some of America's national parks below. Find the meaning of each underlined word and place the letter of the answer in the blank.

_______ **1.** Sequoia National Park in California has <u>majestic</u> giant trees.

_______ **2.** Arches National Park in Utah has tall stone <u>arches</u> and towers.

_______ **3.** Big Bend National Park in Texas has high mountains and deep <u>basins</u>.

_______ **4.** Carlsbad Caverns National Park in New Mexico has millions of bats living in the <u>caverns</u>.

_______ **5.** Everglades National Park in Florida has <u>vicious</u> alligators.

_______ **6.** Yosemite National Park in California has great <u>torrents</u> crashing down.

_______ **7.** Yellowstone National Park in Wyoming has steaming <u>geysers</u>.

_______ **8.** Mesa Verde National Park in Colorado has <u>ruins</u> from old Native American tribes.

_______ **9.** Grand Canyon National Park in Arizona has deep, <u>sheer</u> canyons.

_______ **10.** Denali National Park in Alaska has grizzly bears and <u>caribou</u>.

_______ **11.** Olympic National Park in Washington has miles of Pacific <u>coastline</u>.

_______ **12.** Lassen Volcanic National Park in California has an empty <u>crater</u> at the top of the mountain.

Word Box

a. caves	**e.** great and wonderful	**i.** low and round areas
b. mean and dangerous	**f.** hot springs of water	**j.** waterfalls
c. ancient building remnants	**g.** curved structures	**k.** type of deer
d. steep-walled	**h.** beach and shore	**l.** volcano's hole

Name ______________________________ Date ______________

Two Boys, Two Cultures

Read the following story. Then answer the questions.

Alfred is a member of the Zulu tribe. He and his family live in rural South Africa. They live in a mud house. There is no electricity in the house, so they use candles and oil-burning lamps. A common meal in Alfred's home is cornmeal mush called *iphalishi.* For dessert, there is pumpkin pudding. Meat is expensive, so Alfred rarely has it, but chicken is a special treat. It is very hot and dry in South Africa. Alfred wears shorts even in the winter. Alfred wears a uniform when he goes to school. He learns reading, writing, English, and math, among other subjects. When he grows up, he hopes to work in the city and earn many *rands.*

Ivan lives in urban Russia. He lives with his family in an apartment with three rooms. Ivan's family owns a radio and a small television. A common meal for Ivan is pancakes and bread. Meat is expensive, but chicken is a special treat. It is often very cold and windy in Russia, and in the winter, they get lots of snow. Ivan wears a school uniform and attends third grade. He learns reading, writing, math, and English. When he grows up, he wants to be an engineer and earn many *rubles.*

Circle true or false to answer each question.

1.	Both Alfred and Ivan live on the same continent.	**true**	**false**
2.	Both Alfred and Ivan like to watch television.	**true**	**false**
3.	A typical meal for both boys includes food made from grain.	**true**	**false**
4.	Meat is expensive for both Alfred's and Ivan's families.	**true**	**false**
5.	Both Alfred and Ivan use money called *rands.*	**true**	**false**
6.	Both boys wear uniforms to school.	**true**	**false**
7.	Alfred likes chicken, but Ivan doesn't.	**true**	**false**
8.	Ivan wears shorts in the wintertime.	**true**	**false**
9.	Ivan and Alfred both live in the country.	**true**	**false**
10.	*Iphalishi* is a special Russian dish.	**true**	**false**

Name ______________________ Date __________

Paradise

Imagine an island surrounded by deep-blue seas, covered with lush green plants and brilliant colored flowers. A cool Pacific breeze carries the smell of flowers and the ocean water to you as you relax on a warm, sandy beach. Add to that the sounds of plunging waterfalls and tropical birds. These are the sights and sounds of a paradise called Hawaii.

The beautiful islands of Hawaii make up the youngest member of the United States. Hawaii joined the union on August 21, 1959. It is located in the middle of the Pacific Ocean, far from the mainland of the continental U.S. It is also the southernmost state, reaching latitudes as far south as central Mexico.

Hawaii consists of a chain of 122 volcanic islands, eight of which are considered its main islands. All of the people of Hawaii live on seven of these eight islands. Honolulu, Hawaii's capital, is located on the island of Oahu. Oahu is home to over three-fourths of Hawaii's population.

Hawaii, nicknamed the Aloha State, has unique traditions and friendly people. *Aloha* means love in the Hawaiian language. Islanders often greet tourists with a garland of strung flowers called a *lei*. Visitors also enjoy delicious food, ukulele music, and hula dancing at popular feasts called *luaus*. Many of these customs are the traditions of the Pacific Islanders, called Polynesians, who were the original settlers of Hawaii.

Today, Hawaii is a melting pot of many nationalities and racial groups. Hawaii's population includes people of Polynesian, Chinese, Filipino, and Japanese descent.

Whether a native Hawaiian or a visitor from anywhere around the globe, most would agree that Hawaii is a little slice of heaven on earth.

Name ______________________ Date ____________

Paradise (cont.)

Refer to the passage on page 24 to complete the Venn diagram. Compare and contrast the state of Hawaii with the state in which you live. (Hawaii residents may compare two islands.) Compare and contrast climate, size, people, and geographic features.

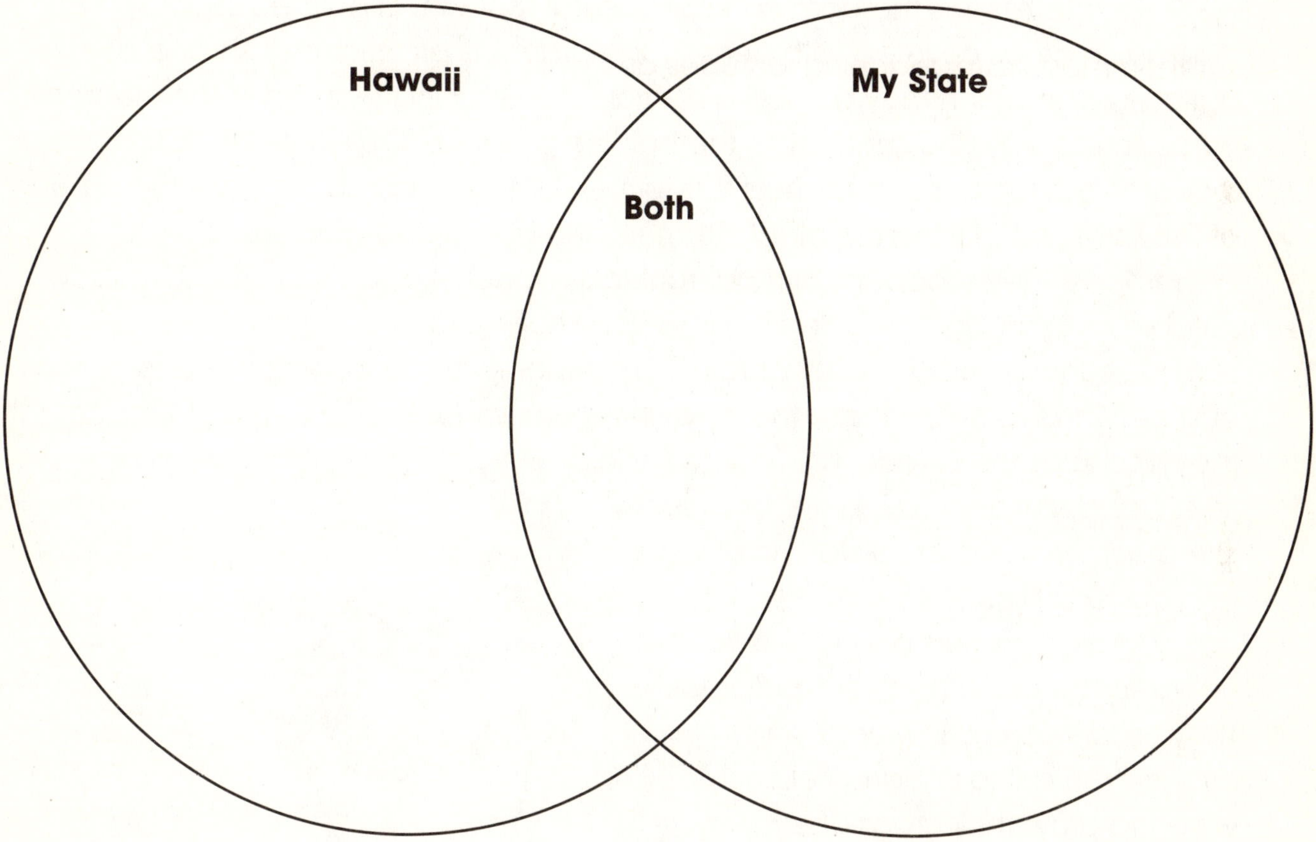

Name ______________________________ Date ______________

Ancient Farming

Three ancient civilizations in the Americas were the Incan, the Aztec, and the Mayan civilizations. The Maya thrived in the area we know as Mexico's Yucatan peninsula and Central America. The Incan empire was located along the west coast of South America in the area known today as Peru and Chile. The Aztec lived in the area we know today as Mexico. Their capital city was in the same place as modern-day Mexico City. Agriculture was very important to all of these civilizations.

For the Aztecs, the common agricultural tool was a pointed stick used for digging. In areas covered with dense forest, farmers practiced slash-and-burn agriculture, in which they burned a section of forest and planted in the cleared areas. In this way, the ashes from the burning produced highly fertile soil. In hilly or mountainous regions, the farmers cut terraces into the hills to increase the amount of flat farmland in which to plant. Farmers also built island-gardens, called *chinampas*. They scooped up mud from lake bottoms and made islands that were suitable for planting. The chinampas yielded huge crops.

The Inca used a variety of farming methods. Along the coastal desert, they built networks to help irrigate the land. In mountainous areas, they cut terraces into the hillsides as the Aztecs did. Their farm fields were divided into three groups. One field was dedicated to the needs of local people. The other two supported state and religious activities.

Mayan farmers built raised fields similar to the chinampas of the Aztecs. They used swampy lowlands and drained the soil to unearth fields on which to grow their crops. They combined this technique with terracing to provide food to feed large populations.

0-7424-1945-2 — *Using the Standards*

Name ______________________ Date ____________

Ancient Farming (cont.)

Answer the questions based on your reading of the passage on page 26.

1. Why do you think agriculture may have been so important to these ancient civilizations?

____

____

2. Why did slash-and-burn agriculture produce highly fertile soil?

____

____

3. Why do you think the chinampa farms of the Aztecs yielded large crops?

____

____

4. List one other reason why terracing might have been helpful to these ancient civilizations.

____

____

5. The farming techniques of all three civilizations are similar even though the people lived in different areas. List two reasons why this might be.

____

____

0-7424-1945-2 — *Using the Standards*

Name ______________________________ Date ______________

Write Now

Genre means a type of writing with characteristics you can recognize. Biographies, science fiction, poetry, and fantasy are all examples of genres.

Circle the correct answer to identify each genre.

1. A story set on another planet would probably be

science fiction biography historical fiction

2. A book of haiku written in the fifteenth century would be

drama poetry adventure

3. A book set in New Orleans during the American Civil War would most likely be

fairy tale fantasy historical fiction

4. A book about the life of Martin Luther King, Jr. would be

poetry biography mystery

5. A book with talking animals as characters would probably be

biography adventure folktale

Write the genre next to each title.

6. *Cinderella* ____________________

7. *Middle School on Mars* ____________________

8. *The Life of Sitting Bull* ____________________

9. *The Knight and the Dragon* ____________________

10. *Rhymes for All Seasons* ____________________

Name ______________________ Date ____________

I Plant

Read the poem and answer the questions below.

I have planted a memory tree,
neither too great
nor too small.
A tree for life,
to celebrate the beauty around me
and to remind me.

May this tree of life I have set to earth
grow roots strongly anchored,
grow branches stretching wide,
to remind me often
of a grandparent's arms
and that loving embrace.

1. Write a summary of the poet's message.

____

____

2. What does the poet remember?

____

____

3. What is the poet celebrating?

____

4. Which word in the poem is a synonym for *secured*?

____

5. Which words show the poet is joyful?

____

Name ______________________________ Date ______________

Matchmaker

Match each set of detail sentences in the left column with its summary statement in the box to the right.

_______ **1.** The children groaned when we woke them so early.
My wife brought a blanket to sit on the ground.
The sun appeared over the treetops.
It was a magnificent sight to see.

_______ **2.** This activity teaches responsibility and caring for others.
Limited space is needed to raise rabbits.
Raising rabbits is an excellent opportunity to teach economics to children.
There is a good market for the sale of domesticated rabbits.

_______ **3.** We arrived at the gates before the fair opened.
The weather stayed cool and sunny all day long.
Our whole family rode lots of rides without having to wait in long lines.
The animal exhibition showcased the best farm animals from our state.

_______ **4.** Mom spent three hours preparing lasagna for dinner.
Dad kept opening the saucepan and sampling the sauce.
All six of us had two helpings of lasagna.
There were no leftovers to freeze for lunches.

_______ **5.** Tadas carefully laid out a plan for each section of his garden.
The hardware store where he bought gardening supplies was crowded.
It took five days to fully prepare the garden plot.
Tadas weeds the garden every Saturday morning.

a. Having a garden can be very time consuming.
b. Raising rabbits is a valuable experience for children.
c. This year's trip to the state fair was lots of fun.
d. The new lasagna recipe was a hit with the whole family.
e. The sunrise that my family experienced was spectacular.

Name ______________________ Date ____________

A Polaroid Moment

Read the cartoon, then answer the questions below.

1. Which of the following best summarizes the cartoon?
  - **a.** A father lovingly pushes his daughter on a swing.
  - **b.** A daughter blames her father for his accidental wipeout.
  - **c.** A father swings his daughter and pays a dear price.

2. In this cartoon, what is meant by an underdog?

____

3. How does the artist portray the girl's happiness?

____

4. Write three words that mean the same as joy.

____

____

____

5. Why might the mother take a picture of this scene?

____

6. Write another title for this comic strip.

____

Name ______________________________ Date ______________

King Tut's Tomb

"King Tut" is the shortened name for a young king, or pharaoh, who ruled ancient Egypt. Tutankhamen (toot-un-CAH-muhn) became king around 1350 B.C. at about the age of nine. Because he became king at such a young age, King Tutankhamen's advisors were more powerful than he was. Not much is known about the life and reign of the teenage ruler; he died when he was only about 18 years old.

King Tut was buried in a tomb located in the Valley of the Kings near the ancient Egyptian city of Thebes. Many ancient Egyptian kings were buried in the Nile Valley in tombs cut into the rocks. Each tomb had several rooms. One room was designed for the dead king's body. Others were used for storing weapons, jewelry, furniture, food, musical instruments, and many other treasures, some of solid gold.

Archaeologists have found many tombs to be empty. Over the centuries, Egyptian tomb robbers and other thieves stole the great treasures that once filled these tombs. Except for the tomb of King Tut, most other tombs have been invaded by thieves.

In 1922, British archaeologist Howard Carter, Lord Carnarvon, and a team of workers uncovered the sealed door of King Tutankhamen's tomb. Beyond the sealed door they found a passageway leading to another door. With great excitement, Carter broke through the second door. Once inside, they were amazed by what they saw. The king's tomb was filled with beautiful treasures! It contained King Tut's golden funeral mask, statues, thrones, chests, chariots, jewelry, ivory game boards, weapons, and model boats, among other objects. There were more than 5,000 items in all. Many of these treasures are on display in the Cairo Museum. Also buried with the king were his two stillborn daughters and a lock of hair from his grandmother, Queen Tiye.

The treasures found in King Tutankhamen's tomb have helped solve some of the mysteries of the lifestyles of royalty in ancient Egypt. Archaeologists continue to search for other undisturbed tombs containing clues to the past.

Name ______________________ Date ____________

King Tut's Tomb (cont.)

Write an F for fact and an O for opinion on the line before each statement. Refer to the passage on page 32.

_______ **1.** Archaeologists have very exciting jobs.

_______ **2.** King Tut's tomb was filled with the most beautiful treasures ever uncovered.

_______ **3.** Tomb robbers have stolen treasures from most of the ancient tombs.

_______ **4.** King Tut was too young to be a good king.

_______ **5.** King Tut was about 18 years old when he died.

_______ **6.** Tutankhamen is a difficult name to pronounce.

_______ **7.** Ancient Egypt was ruled by pharaohs.

_______ **8.** Archaeologists continually search for information about the past.

_______ **9.** Egyptian pharaohs were buried in the Valley of the Kings.

_______ **10.** It would be fun to be a young king like King Tut.

List the advantages and disadvantages of being a king of a powerful kingdom at your age.

Advantages	**Disadvantages**
____________________	____________________
____________________	____________________
____________________	____________________

Name ______________________ Date ______________

Welcome to Our Assembly

Match each one of the statements overheard in a school assembly to the correct student. Pay attention to the character descriptions.

a. Tony Brown—very nervous

b. Abby McMann—observant

c. Percy Pennyfeather—nosy, a busybody

d. Nadia Kosak—arrogant, scheming

e. Jodhi Amani—relieved

f. Jamal Davis—disappointed

g. Mary Marshall—serious, in charge

h. Chang Lee—hopeful, talented

1. ______ "Quiet down, students! We have something important to discuss. I need your attention."

2. ______ "Oh, no! Do you think this is about that prank we pulled at recess?"

3. ______ "Never! We are much too smart to ever get caught!"

4. ______ "That's what you think! I heard all about your trick in the hall! You are in BIG trouble."

5. ______ "I think this is about that science award. I think I could win. My project turned out well."

6. ______ "Look! There's that new teacher. I bet this assembly is to welcome her."

7. ______ "Whew! That was close, you guys! It's good that you didn't get caught."

8. ______ "I thought Chang was going to get that award today. Too bad!"

Name ________________________________ Date ______________

Have I Got a Job for You

Read the five job opportunities below. Match each job applicant with jobs below by writing the correct numbers on each line. Some applicants will have one match and some will have two.

1. Bakers Wanted. Must know flour from powdered sugar. Ability to read is required. Must be 18 years or older. Call Bun in the Oven at 267-1010. Ask for Rose.

2. Yard Work. Like to work up a sweat? Eager to work with loud machines? We've got many positions for hardworking men. Call Hulk at 268-8760.

3. Candy Sales. Sugar-N-Spice is looking for door-to-door sales reps willing to work strictly on commission. Must be a least 16 years old. $100 deposit on first order of candy. Call 1-800-GOCANDY.

4. Child Care. Looking for a 12- to 16-year-old girl to care for my precious 3-year-old. Must love children and ferrets. Need for evening care. Call Mommy at 264-9800.

5. Photogenic? We need students ages 7–14 to model for our Fall Series Clothing Sale. Must have no police record. For the required parental permission form write: P.O. Box 9009, Good Pose, IA 50014.

__________ Tad—14-year-old boy, has no money

__________ Blanche—16-year-old girl, hates noise

__________ Anselm—19-year-old man, cannot read

__________ Zoe—18-year-old woman, won't work door-to-door

__________ Perry—17-year-old female, doesn't know baking ingredients

Name ______________________ Date ____________

The Right Cause

Look at the four causes in the boxes. Find the effects on page 37 that match each of the causes and write them in the balloons.

Captain Colossal is the strongest human on Earth.

My sister is so kind!

Ben is sure he saw a UFO.

Name ______________________ Date ____________

The Right Cause (cont.)

a. grabbed flashlight and blankets

b. has never been beaten in wrestling

c. looks up at the sky every night

d. punches holes in titanium with his fist

e. is afraid to look under the bed

f. volunteers to baby-sit for free

g. dashed to our cellar

h. called everyone together

i. can pick up Neanderthal Nate

j. no one believes a word he says

k. helps me with homework

l. all my friends love her

Name ______________________________ Date ______________

Theme

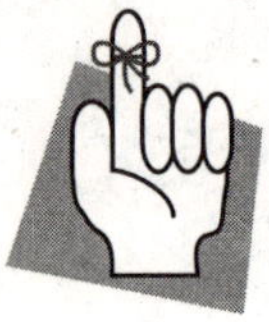

The **theme** is a statement about life—what generally happens in life under specific circumstances. It is not a statement about what should happen. In fiction, the theme unfolds throughout the story and should not be confused with the **moral**, which is made in statements containing words such as *should, ought,* and *must*.

State whether each of the following sentences is a theme or a moral.

1. Teenagers who join many different activities are happy. __________
2. Teenagers who are active should be happy. __________
3. Young people often make poor choices when faced with peer pressure. __________
4. Young people should think carefully when faced with peer pressure. __________
5. People must help others to be good citizens. __________
6. People who help others often feel good about themselves. __________
7. Think of a theme statement around which you could write a story.

____

Clarify your theme by drawing pictures to portray it. Use the following sequence strip to draw your pictures.

Now write the story. Exchange your story with a classmate and write them statements for each other's stories. See whether the statement matches your original theme statement.

Standards in Language Arts

Along with developing reading skills comes the understanding that language is indeed an art. The National Council of Teachers of English (NCTE) standards for language arts can be found at: **www.ncte.org/standards**. From the earliest writings of the young student to the more sophisticated arguments of the older student, progress in language arts is measured in terms of mechanics and expression.

Mechanics and Expression

A standards-based language arts curriculum will refine writing skills in students as they create their own works and evaluate the works of others. Students should have a solid grasp of the following language conventions:

- capitalization and punctuation
- spelling
- sentence structure
- grammar and usage

Students should repeatedly practice the steps of the writing process—prewriting, draft, editing/revising, and publishing. Collect portfolios of student work from prewriting to publishing so students have a firm grasp not only of the effort involved in creative writing, but also the joys of the end result. A published collection of class projects is a wonderful way to share the work of your students with parents and schoolmates.

Hot Tip

Copycat Writing. Let your students learn from the best writers around. As part of your reading time, have students pick out their favorite part of a story. Choose a sentence or two to look at as a class. Write them on the board. Talk about why that sentence is effective and what techniques the author used. Then encourage your students to be copycats. Can they write a sentence of their own using the author's sentence as a model? Make a "copycat corner" in your room, displaying the author's original along with your students' versions.

As students learn the techniques that go into the craft of putting words together, they will begin to see language as an art and seek out that art in their own reading and writing.

Activity List

Activities that allow fifth graders to look more closely at what they already know can be helpful in developing skills in language arts. Students can take apart the parts of a sentence (Activity 1), or use word parts to put sentences back together (Activity 2). Experimenting with sentence placement helps students to grasp the importance of topic and supporting sentences (Activity 3). Students should also continue their use of common reference tools, such as the dictionary, to help language skills in spelling and vocabulary (Activity 4).

Activity 1–Will the Real Verb Please Stand Up?

Standards: Recognizing parts of a sentence, recognizing complete sentences
Goal: Students will practice identifying the complete subject and predicate of various sentences.
Materials: You will need a series of sentences for students to identify; these can come from your class textbook or another age-appropriate selection.
Activity: Although diagramming sentences is considered by many to be an old-fashioned way of teaching language, I like to have students identify the complete subject and predicate by circling the subject and putting a box around the predicate. To help students find the complete subject and predicate, encourage them to first find the verb phrase. Then ask "who?" or "what?" and that will be the complete subject.

Example: The main attraction at the zoo (complete subject) is the monkey cages (predicate).

Activity 2–Mix and Match Noun and Verb Stories

Standards: Using simple and compound sentences, recognizing complete sentences
Goal: Students will construct sentences using noun and verb phrases.
Materials: You will need paper for students and a board to write responses.
Activity: Have each student write a noun and a verb phrase on a piece of paper. List all of these on the board. Have each student write a short paragraph using one of the nouns and one of the verbs. Then give each student a new noun and verb and ask her/him to read the paragraph aloud, substituting the original noun and verb for new ones. These stories can be quite funny, and students enjoy this kind of writing.

Example:

nouns	**verb phrases**
man	found some gold
boy	ate a sweet potato pie
woman	dug a deep hole
girl	ate some cookies

Activity List

Activity 3–Paragraph Puzzle

Standards: Identifying topic sentences for paragraphs, identifying supporting sentences for paragraphs
Goal: Students will reconstruct a paragraph, correctly placing the topic sentence and supporting sentences.
Materials: Create a cut-up paragraph for each student or group of students.
Activity: Take a paragraph from a textbook or other work that you have been using as a class. Choose a paragraph that has a clearly stated topic sentence with supporting sentences (nonfiction passages work best). Retype the paragraph in a large-sized font, with extra spaces between each line. Then cut up the paragraph into pieces—one piece per sentence. Place the pieces of the "puzzle" in an envelope and give to each group of students. Their task is to figure out which piece of the puzzle is the topic sentence. When they have found it, they should reconstruct the paragraph with the other sentences so that it makes sense.

Activity 4–Dictionary Safari

Standards: Using reference tools
Goal: Students will refine dictionary skills by answering a series of questions.
Materials: You will need a dictionary for each student or group of students.
Activity: Play this game by putting a list of questions on the board. The individual or group that finds the answers in their dictionary first is declared the winner. Some sample questions follow. (Answers may vary.)

1. What is the first word in your dictionary? (a)
2. In your dictionary, how many different meanings are listed for the word *fin*? (5)
3. In your dictionary, what word comes after *logic*? (logical)
4. How many pages are there in your dictionary?
5. How many words begin with the letter "x" in your dictionary?
6. What is the last word in your dictionary? (zymurgy)

Name ______________________ Date ____________

Sample Test

Circle the punctuation mark that is needed in the sentence.

1. The team carried in the bats balls and gloves.
- **a.** ;
- **b.** ,
- **c.** :
- **d.** .

2. Come on over," replied Timothy.
- **a.** "
- **b.** ;
- **c.** ,
- **d.** !

3. Did you read that book yet
- **a.** .
- **b.** ,
- **c.** ?
- **d.** ;

4. "Look out" she exclaimed.
- **a.** !
- **b.** ?
- **c.** ;
- **d.** ,

Choose the answer that shows correct capitalization and punctuation.

5. School is in session from ________
- **a.** september through june!
- **b.** September, through June.
- **c.** September through June?
- **d.** September through June.

6. I am interested in buying stickers, ________ the best.
- **a.** and yours are
- **b.** and your's are
- **c.** and yours' are
- **d.** and yours, are

7. I was surprised by what I had ________ would ever believe me.
- **a.** found; No one
- **b.** found? No one
- **c.** found, no one
- **d.** found. No one

8. We went on a field trip to the Art Institute in ________.
- **a.** Chicago, illinois
- **b.** chicago, Illinois
- **c.** Chicago Illinois
- **d.** Chicago, Illinois

GO

Name ______________________ Date ____________

Sample Test (cont.)

Identify the type of writing you would use for each situation.

9. You buy a new game and discover that several pieces are broken. You want to get a replacement.
a. business letter
b. announcement
c. story
d. essay

10. Your teacher asks you to write about an imaginary place.
a. business letter
b. announcement
c. story
d. essay

Choose the word or phrase that best completes the sentence.

11. Cheryl is ________ than I am.
a. more hungrier
b. hungriest
c. most hungry
d. hungrier

12. Tomorrow, I ________ my friend.
a. to meet
b. will meet
c. meets
d. met

13. Juan Carlos taught ________ to play the guitar.
a. hisself
b. itself
c. themselves
d. himself

14. They ________ only two days to go until the science fair.
a. hads
b. haves
c. had
d. half

GO

0-7424-1945-2 — *Using the Standards*

Name ______________________ Date ____________

Sample Test (cont.)

Read the passage. Then answer the questions.

a. Colonies of ants take over the world, proving that these creatures are smarter than man! Nests of these giant insects cover the world's largest cities! Humans everywhere wonder in horror if ants have given up on picnics and are now going for humans!

b. An ant is much more than a little insect carrying breadcrumbs back to its colony. There are more than 8,000 species of ants that exist, with half a million or more members to a colony. And, while they may be nuisances at picnics, ants serve as our "environmental police."

c. For some reason, there is an odd relationship between ants and beetles. Beetles love ants, and frequently live with them in their colonies. The beetles can be "freeloaders" in the ants' home, acting as parasites. At times, they are helpful guests to their hosts, and at other times, they are of no benefit at all and are almost invisible.

d. So, whenever you see a colony of these little creatures, don't sell them short. Think of everything these insects do to help the human species. Marvel at their interesting lives!

15. Which paragraph would be the best opener for a factual story on ants?
- **a.** paragraph a
- **b.** paragraph b
- **c.** paragraph c
- **d.** paragraph d

16. Which paragraph would make the best closing for a factual story on ants?
- **a.** paragraph a
- **b.** paragraph b
- **c.** paragraph c
- **d.** paragraph d

17. Paragraph "a" would be great for—
- **a.** a commercial for picnic baskets.
- **b.** an ad for a documentary on ants.
- **c.** an ending for the story on ants.
- **d.** an ad for a fictional movie about ants.

GO

Name ______________________ Date ____________

Sample Test (cont.)

Choose the answer that best combines the two sentences.

18. The computer is working.
I can't connect to the Internet.
a. I can't connect to the Internet if the computer is working.
b. I can't connect to the Internet with the computer.
c. The computer is working, so I can't connect to the Internet.
d. The computer is working, but I can't connect to the Internet.

19. We raked the leaves yesterday.
The wind blew the leaves off the trees.
a. Yesterday, we raked the leaves that the wind blew off the trees.
b. The wind blew the leaves up the trees, so we raked them up yesterday.
c. The leaves, that we raked were blown.
d. We raked the leaves yesterday and the wind blew the leaves off the trees.

20. My mom knit me a new scarf.
The scarf is blue with green stripes.
a. The blue scarf with green stripes was knit by my mom.
b. My mom knit me a new scarf that is blue with green stripes.
c. My mom, who knit the scarf that is blue with green stripes.
d. My mom knit me a scarf that is blue, green, and new.

Choose the answer that has a spelling error. If there is no mistake, choose the last answer.

21. a. reciept
b. recite
c. reason
d. no mistakes

22. a. auction
b. caught
c. autum
d. no mistakes

23. a. sleigh
b. receive
c. retrieve
d. no mistakes

24. a. enough
b. weather
c. thier
d. no mistakes

STOP

Name ______________________________ Date ______________

Pen Pals

Read the letters. Then do the exercises on page 47.

Dear Yena,

My name is Li Lui. I am 10 years old. I live in Beijing, China. My parents and I live in a tall apartment building. Our city has more than 14 million people. It is a busy city with crowded sidewalks and lots to do.

I like school. I attend from 7:00 A.M. until 4:30 P.M. My favorite subjects are art and Chinese. I don't like math at all, but I have to study it every day! I wear a blue school uniform that looks like a warm-up suit.

I love drawing, watching TV, and eating. My favorite shows are cartoons. My favorite food is shrimp chips. We eat a lot of rice, fish, and vegetables. We eat fish for breakfast to start the day with protein for strength. I like to drink soda.

When I grow up, I'd like to be a fashion designer. I want to design beautiful clothes for famous people to wear. Then, when I go to the movies I can say, "I created that outfit!"

I'm glad to have a pen pal from another country. I hope you are having a nice day! Please write soon.

Sincerely,

Li Lui

Dear Li Lui,

Thank you for writing! I am excited to have a pen pal from China. Your country seems exotic to me. I live in Accra, the capital of Ghana. My home is a one-floor house on a quiet street. I live with my parents and grandmother.

I enjoy school most of the time. My favorite subject is science. I want to be a pediatrician when I grow up, so I can help heal sick children. I'm not so good at French. I need to practice more, but I find it so dull! I wear a uniform to school, too. It's a brown dress with a yellow shirt.

My favorite television programs are cartoons, too. Maybe we watch the same shows. Do you like "Scooby Doo"? I do! I love to eat plantains. They're similar to bananas. I could eat them all day! I eat a lot of rice, also. I like fruit juice better than soda, though.

We have lots in common! I hope you are doing well, and I look forward to your reply.

Sincerely,

Yena

Name ______________________________ Date ______________

Pen Pals (cont.)

Fill in the webs with information from the pen pal letters on page 46. Write Li Lui's information on the left and Yena's information on the right. Draw stars next to the answers they have in common.

Li Lui | **Yena**

where they live
- house
- city
- country

what they like
- TV show
- food
- drink

school
- uniform
- favorite subject
- least favorite subject

0-7424-1945-2 — *Using the Standards*

Name ______________________ Date ______________

Audience and Purpose

Having the same **purpose** but a different **audience** affects writing. For example, your purpose is to address the parking problem in the downtown area of a small city. Lack of parking lots has caused car owners to park dangerously close to other cars, to block entranceways, and to avoid the downtown area during busy shopping times.

Describe the problem above to each of the following audiences:

1. Shoppers ______________________

____

2. City police ______________________

____

3. Store owners ______________________

____

4. Pedestrians ______________________

____

How has changing the audience affected your writing? Discuss your changes in a small group.

Name ______________________________ Date ______________

Topic Sentences

Topic sentences state the main idea of the paragraph. Although most topic sentences appear at the beginning of the paragraph, some writers place them at the end or even in the middle of a paragraph for variety. Other sentences in the paragraph contribute to the topic sentence in some way. Topic sentences help readers by preparing them for what lies ahead. If the topic sentence does not guide the reader, good writers leave it out. For example, in descriptive paragraphs, chronological events or descriptive details often unify the sentences so a general topic is implied, making a topic sentence unnecessary.

Choose a subject from the list below. List four or five main ideas you will present as you organize your essay. These main ideas will later become topic sentences for the paragraphs within the essay. Use the outline below to list your topic sentence ideas.

- Convince your best friend to try your favorite sport or pastime.
- Encourage the student council to hold an activity night for middle-school students.
- Explain to your parents why you are ready for a part-time job.
- Analyze reasons people your age should do community service.

Subject ______________________________

Main idea 1 ______________________________

Main idea 2 ______________________________

Main idea 3 ______________________________

Main idea 4 ______________________________

Write an essay, using each main idea as a topic sentence that controls the idea for the new paragraph. Use supporting sentences to develop each topic sentence idea.

Name ______________________ Date ____________

Supporting Sentences

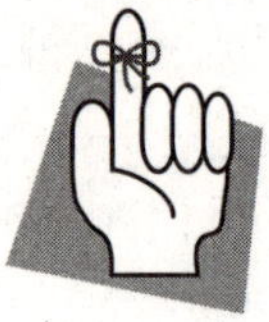

After deciding on a subject and several main points or topics, good writers think about how best to prove their points. To prove topic sentences, **supporting sentences** are needed to convince the reader.

Refer to your list of main ideas from page 49. Choose two to develop. List as many supporting ideas as possible below. If you have more than five supporting ideas, you may need extra space.

Main idea 1 (from page 49) ______________________

Supporting detail ______________________

Supporting detail ______________________

Supporting detail ______________________

Supporting detail ______________________

Supporting detail ______________________

Main idea 2 (from page 49) ______________________

Supporting detail ______________________

Supporting detail ______________________

Supporting detail ______________________

Supporting detail ______________________

Supporting detail ______________________

Continue with the other main ideas on a separate sheet of paper. Then turn all supporting sentence ideas into complete sentences.

Using your outline of main ideas and supporting sentences, turn your notes into an essay. Remember, a topic sentence may be more effective in the middle or at the end of its paragraph.

0-7424-1945-2 — *Using the Standards*

Name ______________________________ Date ______________

Sentence Combining

Combine the following sentences to form compound or complex sentences.

1. Dennis enjoys his creative writing class. The class gives him an opportunity to try writing different types of stories.

2. Writers face problems. Writers can solve problems in group discussions.

3. Mandy enjoys writing poetry. Mandy dislikes writing mystery stories.

4. Proofreaders read for errors. Proofreaders read only after they first edit content.

5. The bases were loaded. Mighty Casey struck out.

Create two sentences of your own. Ask a partner to combine them into either a compound or complex sentence.

In a large group, have volunteers write their sentences on the board. Discuss various ways to combine their sentences. Vote for the best version.

Name ______________________ Date ____________

Identifying Sentences

A **sentence** is a group of words that tells a complete thought.
A **fragment** is not a complete thought.

sentences:	Paris is in France. I went to Tokyo many years ago.
fragments:	The beautiful city of Venice. Because Bombay is so old.

Write sentence on the line before each sentence. Write fragment on the line before each fragment.

1. ______________ Tel Aviv is in Israel.
2. ______________ The ancient cities of Sparta and Athens.
3. ______________ St. Petersburg used to be called Leningrad.
4. ______________ Cape Town is near the Cape of Good Hope.
5. ______________ Because no one lives in the city of Machu Picchu.
6. ______________ The town of Alice Springs lies in the middle of Australia.

Read the paragraph. Underline the fragments. Then, rewrite the fragments to make complete sentences. (Hint: Sometimes you can fix a fragment by making it part of another sentence.)

Pamplona is a city in northern Spain. A very old city. Every year, the city hosts a celebration. Bulls are set free to run through the city streets. People come from around the world to run through the streets with the bulls. Because running with the bulls can be dangerous. People are sometimes hurt.

7. ____

____

8. ____

____

Name ______________________________ Date ______________

Compound Subjects and Predicates

A **compound subject** is made up of two subjects joined by the word **and**. Sentences with the same predicate may be joined by using a compound subject.

Example: Mice are a kind of mammal.
Humans are a kind of mammal.
Mice and humans are kinds of mammals.

A **compound predicate** is made up of two predicates joined by the word **and**. Sentences with the same subject may be joined by using a compound predicate.

Example: Mice can climb well. Mice can run quickly.
Mice can climb well and run quickly.

Combine these sentences using a compound subject.

1. Humans can solve mazes. Mice can solve mazes.

____

2. Mice like to eat cheese. Humans like to eat cheese.

____

Combine these sentences using a compound predicate.

3. Humans are able to reason. Humans are able to speak.

____

4. Mice eat in their nests. Mice sleep in their nests.

____

Combine these sentences.

5. Humans care for their babies. Mice care for their babies.

____

6. Mice wake up at night. Mice look for food at night.

____

Name ______________________ Date ____________

Editing Skills

As part of the writing process, you should edit your work. It can be useful to trade papers with a friend and edit each other's work. When you edit, you should look for correct use of capital letters and punctuation, spelling errors, and anything that is unclear or hard to understand.

There are special symbols you can use to edit writing. Use the chart below to helpyou edit the report on page 55. The more you edit, the better your writing will be.

≡	capital letter	Max smith (≡ under s)
/	lowercase letter	We like to ~~E~~at. (e written above)
⊙	add period	It was fun ⊙
?	add question mark	Do you like pizza ?
∧	insert, add this	Ten ∧ were coming. (people written above)
(delete mark)	delete, take out	Jump ~~all~~ around the room.
∨ (with ')	add apostrophe	The bike was Sarahs. (apostrophe inserted before s)
❛❛ ❜❜	add quotation marks	Johnathan yelled, Supper! (quotation marks inserted)
¶	new paragraph	happy. ¶ The boy loved dogs.

Name ______________________________ Date ______________

Editing Skills (cont.)

Autumn is a nice time of year in michigan. some people like to go water-skiing in the summer. Most people enjoy the changes autumn brings. New sounds, sights, and smells arrive with the crisp wind that replaces the soft summer air

Early in the season, many people like two pick Apples and make good apple pies. They is the time of year for enjoying apple cider, donuts, and hayrides. Pumpkin pies make delicious desserts on thanksgiving Day. What is your favorite season Mines definitely autumn!

As the temperatures outside drop, so do the pretty leaves on the trees. Families work together raking they into piles. Children can be heard laughing as he jump into big piles of leaves. Later, the smell of burning leaves often fills the autumn air.

As the autumn air grows even cooler, tree branches begin too look bare under a gray sky. November winds soon whisk away the fallen dried leaves. Michigan says farewell two gentle autumn and hello too the harsh winter that lies ahead.

Name ______________________________ Date ______________

Spelling Practice

For each sentence, find the word that is spelled correctly and fits best in the blank.

1. Nathan __________ the ball.
- **a.** catched
- **b.** cot
- **c.** caught
- **d.** caut

2. Yogurt, milk, and cheese are all __________ products.
- **a.** diary
- **b.** dairy
- **c.** dairey
- **d.** darey

3. The sunset over the mountains was a beautiful __________.
- **a.** scene
- **b.** seen
- **c.** sceen
- **d.** seene

4. That is not a __________ diamond.
- **a.** real
- **b.** reel
- **c.** reale
- **d.** reele

Read the phrases. Choose the phrase in which a word is not spelled correctly.

5.
- **a.** vertical line
- **b.** soft mattres
- **c.** useful example
- **d.** special bubbles

6.
- **a.** our residence
- **b.** final notice
- **c.** usually late
- **d.** not possibel

7.
- **a.** diferent name
- **b.** really tired
- **c.** very unusual
- **d.** go through

8.
- **a.** glove compartmant
- **b.** cold beverage
- **c.** best friend
- **d.** straight line

0-7424-1945-2 — *Using the Standards*

Standards in Math

Standards-based math activities encourage students to explore mathematical processes in different contexts. To begin to implement math standards in your class, a great starting place is the standard framework developed by the National Council of Teachers of Mathematics (NCTM). For more on the NCTM standards, see: **standards.nctm.org**. NCTM divides mathematical standards into the following content strands:

- Number and Operations
- (Pre-)Algebra
- Geometry
- Measurement
- Data Analysis and Probability

The NCTM process strands—Problem Solving, Reasoning and Proof, Connections, Communication, and Representation—describe the different ways that students come to understand and apply mathematical knowledge. Developing a standards-based mathematical curriculum is as much about *how* you teach as *what* you teach. The process strands provide a solid base for understanding *how* to work through content learning.

Problem Solving

Recognizing that students use a variety of processes to get to a solution, teachers should encourage discussion by asking frequently: How did you get that answer? What steps did you take? As students communicate their ideas to others, they understand better the processes they are using and find new tools for problem solving in the strategies of others.

Students should practice solving problems in a variety of contexts—from math equations to story problems about real-life situations. This develops critical thinking skills and provides an answer to that ever-popular question: "When will I use this?"

Reasoning and Proof

Once students have figured out an answer, they should spend a moment reflecting: Does the answer make sense? What tools can be used to prove the answer? Reasoning and proof will vary depending on the level of your students, but there are some basic principles to use for all math situations. Students can draw a picture or use an opposite operation to help them understand not only *if* an answer is true, but also *why*.

Standards in Math

Communication

Students can learn as much from each other as from the teacher when given the chance to organize and explain their work. Seeing how someone else solved a problem may unlock the key of understanding for a student who has been stuck using a different strategy. Encourage students to communicate using their own words, symbols, and mathematical vocabulary. Spend time talking—not just about the answer, but the various ways to get there.

Connections

As students gain mathematical knowledge, it is important to make connections between different branches of mathematics. For example, an understanding of the number system and place value provides the foundation for developing skills in algebra or geometry. Relating mathematics to real-world situations with which students are familiar significantly improves retention and problem-solving abilities. Students develop critical thinking skills when they are able to make predictions, build on previous knowledge, and see the connections between math concepts and the world around them.

Representation

Knowing that math is more than numbers on a page can help students construct meaning in mathematics. Students should be encouraged to represent a problem in a variety of ways. This might involve recognizing the same number whether it is written as a numeral, spoken as a word, or shown with objects. By providing a range of models to choose from, you will give your students the necessary tools to master all branches of mathematics.

Hot Tip

Hands-On Math. If your students are having a hard time understanding a mathematical concept, why not give them a hand? A variety of manipulatives, such as base-ten blocks, linking cubes, or fraction stacks can help students grasp the meaning of math concepts and offer a hands-on way to work with numbers. Some students need to experiment with objects in order to understand mathematical laws and properties.

Applying the process strands when teaching the basic skills for each area of mathematics will empower your students with critical thinking skills applicable to all areas of inquiry and exploration of the world around them.

Activity List

Math problems can be set up as a daily puzzle. They may be written on the board or sent home on slips of paper. As with reading puzzles, math puzzles are also rewarded with a prize. The sampling of activities that follow come from areas of the NCTM standards for math.

Activity 1–Number and Operations

Standards: Estimating

Estimating can be fun, and with practice, students will get good at it. Try some of these estimating activities.

1. Estimate how many leaves on a tree. Count the leaves in a square-foot patch. Use the one-foot sample to estimate the number of leaves on the whole tree.
2. Estimate how many beans will fit in a particular jar. Counting as you work, fill the jar with beans. How close was your estimate?
3. Estimate how many cars are in the school parking lot. Go outside and count them. How close was the estimate?

Activity 2–(Pre-)Algebra

Standards: Recognizing patterns

In each row, look at the number patterns. At the end of each row, write the number that will continue the pattern.

3	4	4	3	4	4	3	4	(4)
1	2	3	1	2	3	1	2	(3)
0	9	0	8	0	7	0	6	(0)
2	4	6	7	2	4	6	7	(2)

Activity 3–Geometry

Standards: Identifying lines of symmetry

Give students an opportunity to explore symmetry with the following exercises.

1. Fold a see-through sheet of paper vertically and unfold it again.
2. Write the capital letters A–Z down the exact middle of the paper. There should be one half of each letter on either side of the fold.
3. Fold the paper in half again.
4. Which letters line up? These are letters with a line of symmetry.
5. Experiment with different shapes to see which have a line of symmetry.

Activity List

Activity 4–Measurement

Standards: Using nonstandard units of measurement

Encourage students to explore using nonstandard units of measurement by using their bodies. A foot or even a thumb can be used as a unit of measurement!

1. Guess how many steps it is to the library. Walk toe to heel and find out how close your estimation was.
2. How many giant steps is the diameter of a baseball diamond? Walk it off and find out. Then figure how many giant steps square is the baseball diamond.
3. Estimate how many thumbs wide your leg is from the knee to your ankle. Then use your thumbs to measure it.

Activity 5–Data Analysis and Probability

Standards: Solving experimental probability situations, graphing data

Put those probability ideas to the test by trying them out. Have students put these situations to the test by doing the activity themselves.

1. How many times would you have to flip a coin to get heads 3 times in a row? Flip a coin 100 times and see how many times you get heads 3 times in a row.
2. If you roll a die 6 times, how many times do you estimate you will roll a 6? Roll a die 60 times and see if you get the number 6 ten times.
3. If you ask 10 friends to pick a number between 0 and 11, how well distributed will the choices be? Try it. Then record the data in a chart or table.

Activity 6–Problem Solving

Standards: Using a variety of methods to solve problems, using appropriate operations

Place +, –, x, or / (fraction sign) in the series of numbers to make true equations.

5	0	1	0	5	(50/10 = 5)
4	5	3	4	8	(45 + 3 = 48)
8	1	8	0	1	(81 – 80 = 1)
3	1	5	4	5	(3 x 15 = 45)

Name ______________________________ Date ______________

Sample Test

Read each problem. Choose the letter with the correct answer.

1. Which is equivalent to 11,568?
a. (10 x 10,000) + (5 x 100) + (6 x 10) + (8 x 1)
b. (1 x 1,000) + (5 x 100) + (6 x 10) + 8 x 1
c. (1 x 10,000) + (1 x 1,000) + (5 x 100) + (6 x 10) + (8 x 1)
d. (11,000 x 1) + (500 x 10) + (60 x 100) + (8 x 1,000)

2. What fraction of the triangles is shaded?

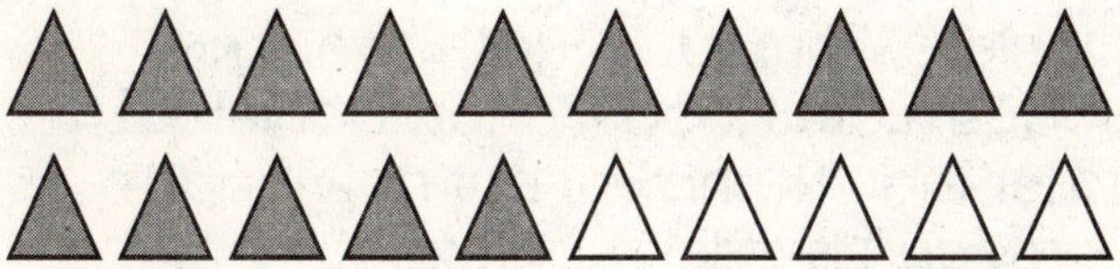

a. $\frac{1}{4}$
b. $\frac{1}{5}$
c. $\frac{4}{5}$
d. $\frac{3}{4}$

3. Which of the statements is true about the numbers in the box?

2, 3, 5, 7, 11, 13, 17

a. They are all even numbers.
b. They are all odd numbers.
c. They are all perfect squares.
d. They are all prime numbers.

4. Kevin drove 300 miles in 5 hours and used 10 gallons of gas. How many miles per hour was he traveling?
a. 60
b. 55
c. 30
d. 70

5. How much sales tax is charged when you buy a shirt that costs $15?

Price of Item	Sales Tax
$1	$0.06
$2	$0.12
$3	$0.18
$4	$0.24

a. $0.06
b. $1.50
c. $15.90
d. $0.90

6. A cash box contains $16.00. All of the coins are either quarters or nickels. There are 20 nickels. How many of the coins are quarters?
a. 30
b. 60
c. 20
d. 40

7. The decimal equivalent of $\frac{1}{8}$ is 0.125.

What is the decimal equivalent of $\frac{5}{8}$?
a. 0.0625
b. 0.058
c. 0.625
d. 0.58

8. Which choice makes this a true statement?

The sum of two odd numbers is—
a. even.
b. prime.
c. odd.
d. positive.

GO

Name ______________________ Date ____________

Sample Test (cont.)

Solve each problem. Choose the letter of the correct answer. Select "none of these" if the correct answer is not given.

9. What is the next number in the number sequence?

3, 7, 11, 15, 19

a. 20
b. 21
c. 23
d. 24
e. none of these

10. What is the rule for this number sequence?

15, 30, 45, 60, 75

a. x 5
b. x 2
c. + 15
d. + 10
e. none of these

11. A function machine produces the following results. Choose the rule that describes the function connecting the IN values to the OUT values.

IN	1	2	3	4	8
OUT	3	6	9	12	24

a. + 1
b. + 3
c. x 2
d. x 4
e. none of these

12. Which values will make the equation true?

$3 + 2x - 4 \div x = y$

a. $x = 2$, $y = 3$
b. $x = 4$, $y = 1$
c. $x = 2$, $y = 6$
d. $x = 4$, $y = 9$
e. none of these

13. Four jets landed at the Kennedy Airport at the same time. Jet 1 carried 460 passengers. Jet 2 carried 15% more passengers than jet 1. How many passengers were on jet 2?

a. 69
b. 529
c. 391
d. 506
e. none of these

14. Danielle, Tamequa, Rashawn, and Joaqu´n are good friends. Danielle is taller than Rashawn, but not Joaqu´n. Tamequa is taller than exactly 2 of the other children. What is the correct order of children, from shortest to tallest?

a. Rashawn, Tamequa, Danielle, Joaqu´n
b. Danielle, Rashawn, Tamequa, Joaqu´n
c. Rashawn, Danielle, Joaqu´n, Tamequa
d. Rashawn, Danielle, Tamequa, Joaqu´n
e. none of these

15. Kiwadin spent \$10 on supplies for his leaf-raking business. He charges \$15 per yard he rakes. Which equation shows the relationship between the number of yards raked, *Y*, and his total profit, *P*?

a. $P = \$10 \times Y$
b. $P = \$15 \times Y + \$10$
c. $P = \$10 \times Y - \$10$
d. $P = \$15 \times Y - \$10$
e. none of these

GO

Name ______________________ Date ______________

Sample Test (cont.)

Choose the letter with the correct answer.

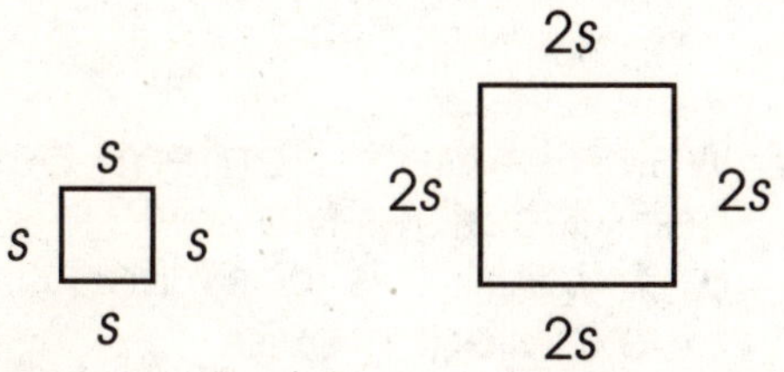

16. Which expression models the area of square 1?
a. $4s$
b. s^2
c. $4s^2$
d. $s + 4$

17. Which expression models the area of square 2?
a. $2s^2$
b. $8s$
c. s^2
d. $4s^2$

18. Which shows a line of symmetry?

a. 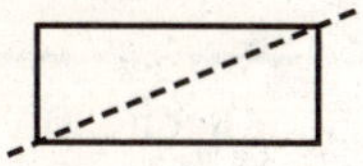

b. 

c. 

d. 

19. A bicycle wheel has a radius of 30 cm. What is the measure of its diameter?
a. 900 π cm
b. 15 cm
c. 60 cm
d. 60 π cm

20. If 1 kg = 2.2 lbs.,how many lbs. is 3.5 kg?
a. 5.7 lbs.
b. 6.0 lbs.
c. 6.6 lbs.
d. 7.7 lbs.

21. About how long is a baseball bat?
a. 3 inches long
b. 3 feet long
c. 3 yards long
d. 3 miles long

22. A bridge has a weight limit of 6,000 pounds. How many tons will the bridge hold?
a. 4 tons
b. 1 ton
c. 3 tons
d. 2 tons

23. 4 gallons =
a. 40 cups
b. 8 quarts
c. 16 pints
d. 64 cups

24. On the Fahrenheit scale, what is the temperature for the freezing point of water?
a. 32°
b. 0°
c. 57°
d. 24°

GO

Name ______________________ Date ____________

Sample Test (cont.)

Twenty people were asked to rate two movies on a scale of 0–5, with 5 being the best. The results are summarized on the graphs below. Use the graphs to answer questions 25–30. Choose the letter with the correct answer.

Movie #1

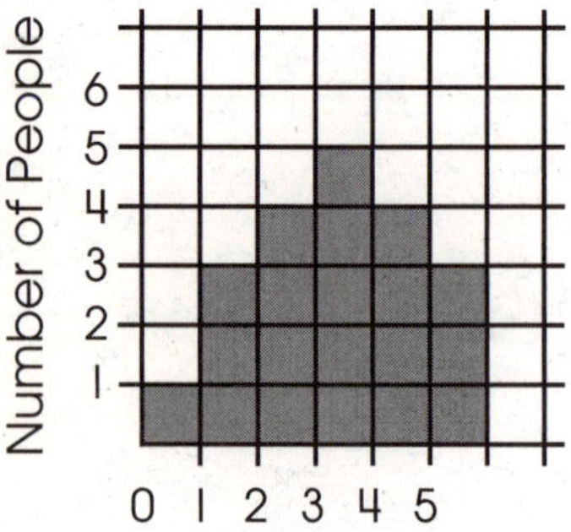

Rating

Movie #2

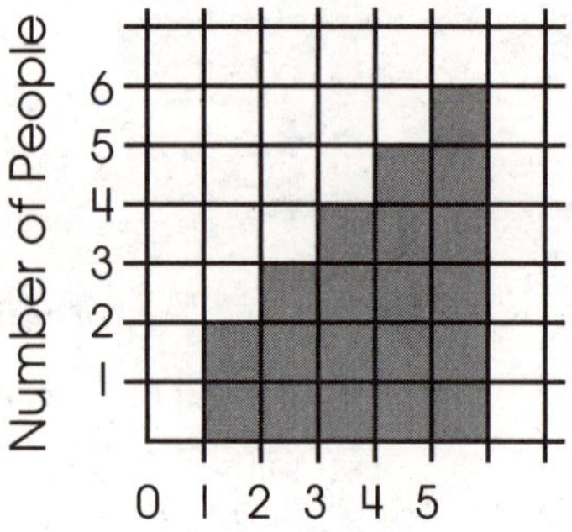

Rating

25. What percentage of the people gave Movie 1 a rating higher than 3?
a. 45%
b. 20%
c. 40%
d. 35%

26. What percentage of the people gave Movie 2 a rating higher than 3?
a. 50%
b. 55%
c. 60%
d. 45%

27. Which gives the best estimate for the mean rating of Movie 1?
a. 1
b. 2
c. 3
d. 4

28. What is the mode rating for Movie 2?
a. 2
b. 3
c. 4
d. 5

29. Which of the statements below best describes Movie 1?
a. Overall, this was rated as an excellent movie.
b. Overall, this was rated an average movie.
c. Overall, this was rated as a terrible movie.
d. Overall, it rated better than Movie 2.

30. Which of the statements below best describes Movie 2?
a. Overall, this was rated as an excellent movie.
b. Overall, this was rated as an average movie.
c. Overall, this was rated as a terrible movie.
d. Overall, it did not rate as well as Movie 1.

---

31. The probability of randomly drawing a blue cube out of a bag is 20%. Which of the following color combinations could be in the bag?
a. 3 red, 4 blue, and 3 yellow
b. 5 red, 2 blue, and 5 yellow
c. 6 red, 3 blue, and 2 yellow
d. 6 red, 2 blue, and 2 yellow

32. You roll a six-sided number cube. What is the probability that you will roll a number less than 4?
a. 1:2
b. 1:3
c. 1:6
d. 5:6

STOP

Name ______________________ Date ____________

Place Value

Write the correct numeral for each number.

1. five hundred sixty-two thousand, one hundred seventy-four

____

2. two hundred million, five hundred eighteen thousand, seven hundred thirty-six

____

3. sixty-five billion, two hundred seventy million, nine hundred forty-eight thousand, three hundred one

____

Match the underlined digit with its place value.

4. ______ 5.7123

5. ______ 208.0023

6. ______ 0.00452

7. ______ 0.0002

8. ______ 1,230.023

9. ______ 265,300.023

a. two hundreds

b. two thousandths

c. two hundred thousandths

d. two hundredths

e. two hundred thousands

f. two ten thousandths

Rearrange the group of numbers from smallest to largest.

10. 712.01, 711.9, 712.10, 712.09, 711.95, 712.001, 711.009

____

Name ______________________________ Date ______________

Number Crunching

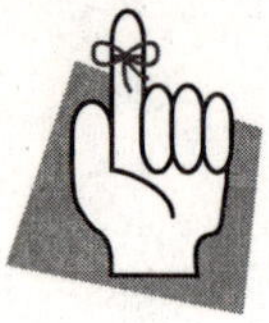

Numbers can be written in three ways.

standard form = 465
expanded form = 400 + 60 + 5
word form = four hundred sixty-five

Middle school students across the country were asked about their favorite after-school snacks. The results are in the chart below.

Favorite Snack	Number of Students
Fruit	25,360,251
Cookies	31,425,620
Sandwich	728,715
Candy	72,815
Popcorn	300,002
Vegetables	19,205

Use the chart to answer the questions below. Write all answers in both expanded and word forms.

1. How many students prefer popcorn?

____

2. How many students prefer the least favorite choice?

____

3. How many students prefer the favorite choice?

____

4. How many total students were surveyed?

____

5. What was the difference between the least favorite choice and the favorite choice?

____

0-7424-1945-2 — *Using the Standards*

Name ______________________ Date ______________

What Number Am I?

Read the clues carefully. Exchange answers with classmates and explain how you solved the problems. Create two problems on the back of this sheet.

1. What number am I?
I am an even number.
I come between 40 and 50.
I do not contain a 0.
Each of my 2 digits is different from the other.
I am not 46 nor 48.

I am ________ .

2. What number am I?
I am an odd number.
I am less than 20.
I am more than 13.
My number does not contain a 9 or a 7.

I am ________ .

3. What number am I?
I am an odd number.
I come between 79 and 89.
One of my digits is a 3.

I am ________ .

4. What number am I?
I can be divided evenly by 2.
I am less than 30.
I am more than 22.
One of my digits is a 6.

I am ________ .

5. What number am I?
I cannot be divided evenly by 2.
I can be divided evenly by 5.
I am less than 77.
I am more than 69.

I am ________ .

Name ______________________ Date ____________

Lines of Integers

Add the positive and negative integers. Illustrate your answer on the number line. The first one has been done for you.

1. $5 + {}^{-}7 =$ ${}^{-}2$

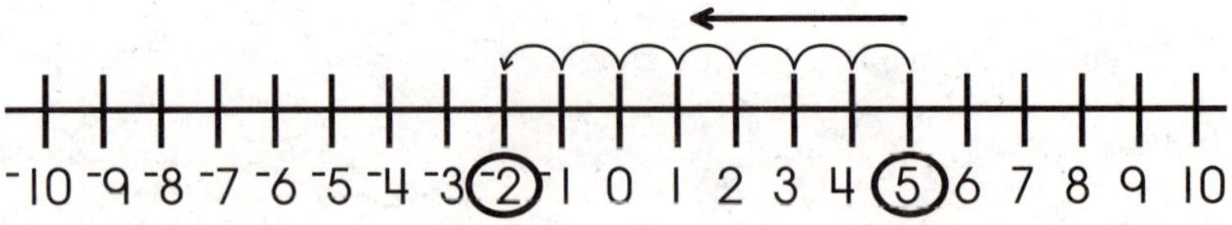

2. $4 + {}^{-}3 =$ ______

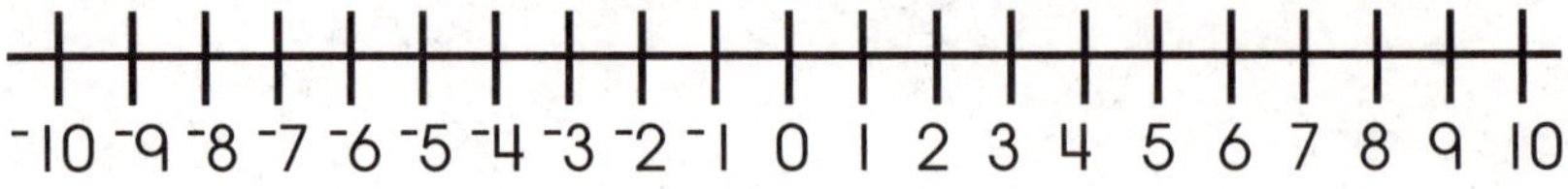

3. $2 + {}^{-}6 =$ ______

4. $3 + {}^{-}5 =$ ______

5. $7 + {}^{-}6 =$ ______

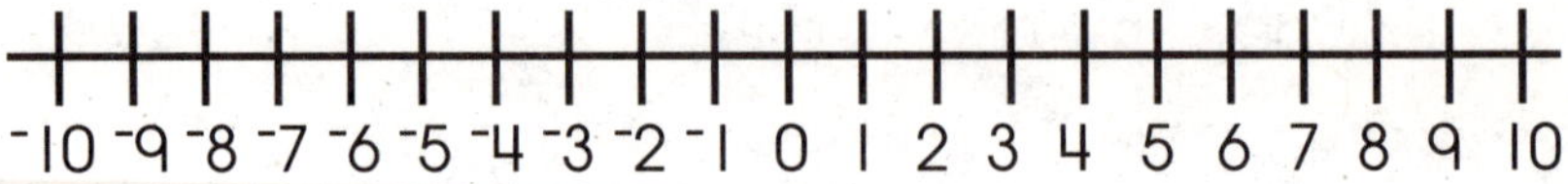

6. $5 + {}^{-}2 =$ ______

7. ${}^{-}6 + {}^{-}3 =$ ______

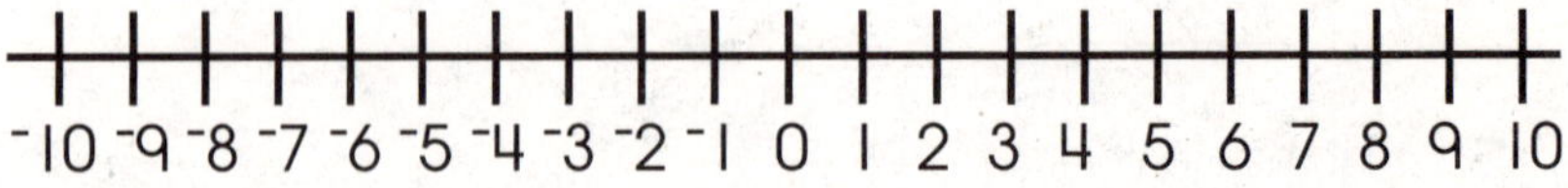

8. $10 + {}^{-}8 =$ ______

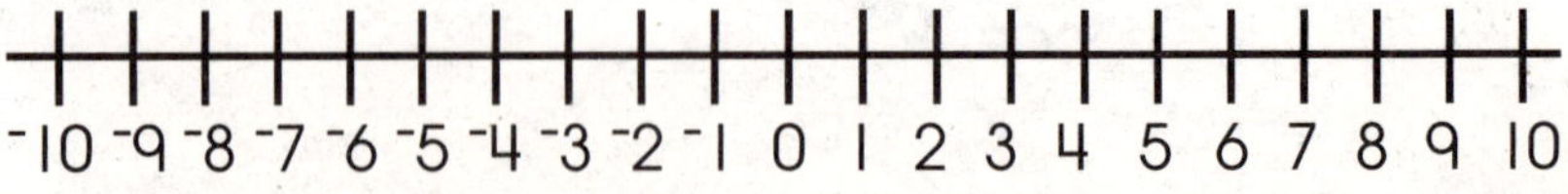

0-7424-1945-2 — *Using the Standards*

Name ______________________ Date ______________

How Long Would It Take?

Think about each problem carefully before you begin to solve it. Compare your answers and the steps used to find them with a small group.

1. News travels fast. Suppose you won $1,000 at 3:00 P.M. If you phoned 2 friends to share the news within 10 minutes of opening the envelope, and if each of those 2 friends called 2 different friends within the next 10 minutes, and this went on until 4:00 P.M., and no one was called more than once, how many friends would know the news by 4:00 P.M.?

____

2. You and your family are on a vacation and must travel 1,210 miles in a car. You average 55 miles per hour. If you stop to rest and eat for exactly 4 hours during this trip and if you leave home at 6:00 in the morning on Monday, at what time and on what day will you reach your destination?

____

3. The sun is about 93,000,000 miles from Earth. Light travels at 186,000 miles per second. About how many minutes does it take light from the sun to reach Earth?

____

4. Tom walked steadily at 2 miles an hour. How long will it take him to walk 7,920 yards?

____

Name ______________________________ Date ______________

Which Is More?

Use your knowledge of mathematical operations to answer the questions.

1. Which is more—

a. 15 boxes of 18 suckers or 12 boxes of 24 chocolate bars?

____

b. How do you know?

____

2. Which is more—

a. 12 bags of 30 buttons or 16 bags of 25 buttons?

____

b. How do you know?

____

3. Which is larger—

a. the rectangular room that is 12 ft. by 14 ft. or the one that is 15 ft. by 11 ft.?

____

b. How do you know?

____

4. What operation did you use to find the answers?

____

Name ______________________ Date ____________

Cycling for Fractions

Aren is making deliveries on his bike. He follows his boss's directions and zigzags across downtown. Add fractions under GO signs and subtract fractions under STOP signs. Write each answer on the line. Find the total at the end of the trip.

1. GO $\frac{3}{4}$
2. STOP $\frac{1}{2}$ ________
3. GO $\frac{1}{4}$ ________
4. STOP $\frac{1}{6}$ ________
5. GO $\frac{1}{3}$ ________
6. STOP $\frac{2}{4}$ ________
7. GO $\frac{4}{6}$ ________
8. STOP $\frac{2}{6}$ ________
9. GO $\frac{5}{9}$ ________
10. STOP $\frac{3}{4}$ ________
11. GO $\frac{1}{6}$ ________
12. STOP $\frac{1}{3}$ ________

________ **Total**

Name ______________________________ Date ______________

Freaky Fractions

$\frac{1}{2} = 0.5$ $\frac{1}{3} \approx 0.33$

$\frac{1}{4} = 0.25$ $\frac{1}{5} = 0.20$

$\frac{1}{6} \approx 0.17$

1. Estimate the decimal equivalent of $\frac{2}{3}$ without using long division or a calculator. Show your work.

2. Estimate the decimal equivalent of $\frac{2}{5}$, $\frac{3}{5}$, and $\frac{4}{5}$ without using long division or a calculator. Show your work.

3. Estimate the decimal equivalent of $\frac{2}{6}$, $\frac{3}{6}$, $\frac{4}{6}$, and $\frac{5}{6}$ without using long division or a calculator. Show your work.

4. Insert the correct sign (**<**, **>**, or **=**) between each pair of fractions.

a. $\frac{2}{3}$ _____ $\frac{3}{5}$ **b.** $\frac{2}{5}$ _____ $\frac{1}{3}$

c. $\frac{3}{4}$ _____ $\frac{4}{5}$ **d.** $\frac{3}{5}$ _____ $\frac{1}{2}$

5. Explain the method you used to solve problem 4. Compare solution methods with your classmates.

Name ____________________ Date __________

Two-Stepping

Solve each word problem.

1. If you buy 2 cheese sandwich lunches at $0.95 each, plus a $0.75 soda, and give the cashier $5.00, how much change should you get back?

____

2. Your teacher treated each of the 27 students in your class to a fast food lunch for $1.95 each, plus 2 lunches for herself. She had $60.00. How much change does she get?

____

3. You bought white milk at $0.25 for 20 days. Your friend bought chocolate milk at $0.35 for 20 days. How much more did your friend spend in all?

____

4. You collected 887 baseball cards. Your friend collected 10 times as many, as well as 34 comic books. How many items did your friend collect?

____

5. The school cook uses 1,440 chocolate chips to make 480 cookies. Each chip costs $0.02. How much does it cost to add chocolate chips to each cookie?

____

6. Each burger is topped with 4 pickles. Each cheeseburger is topped with 2 slices of cheese. If 1 order is placed for 437 burgers, and another order is placed for 758 cheeseburgers, which order will have the most toppings?
How much more?

____

0-7424-1945-2 — *Using the Standards*

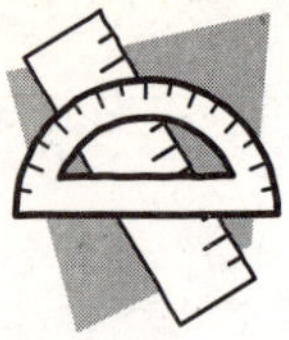

Name ______________________________ Date ______________

School Supplies

The list at the bottom of the page shows the cost of some items at the school store. Round the cost of each item to the nearest dime. Estimate the cost of the following purchases. Write down your estimate. On the back of this paper, add the actual cost of the items and record the sums. Was your estimate close?

1. 1 ruler, 2 pencils, 1 spiral notebook, 1 eraser

My estimate $ ______ Actual cost $ ______

2. A 3-ring binder, 1 ballpoint pen, 1 bottle glue, 2 pencils

My estimate $ ______ Actual cost $ ______

3. 1 box of crayons, 1 box of colored pencils, 1 3-ring binder

My estimate $ ______ Actual cost $ ______

4. 2 folders, 1 spiral notebook, 1 eraser, 1 pencil

My estimate $ ______ Actual cost $ ______

5. 2 ball point pens, 3 folders, 1 ruler, 1 spiral notebook

My estimate $ ______ Actual cost $ ______

6. 1 box of crayons, 1 pencil, 1 eraser, 1 folder

My estimate $ ______ Actual cost $ ______

pencil	$0.28	box of crayons	$1.19
eraser	$0.32	colored pencils	$1.51
folder	$0.49	spiral notebook	$0.69
ruler	$0.91	3-ring binder	$2.98
glue	$1.08	ballpoint pen	$0.62

Name ______________________ Date ____________

Factor Trees

Fill in the factor trees by multiplying. The numbers in the first row are the prime factors of the composite number at the root of the tree.

1.
3 x 3 x 2
☐ x 2
☐

2.
3 x 5 x 3
☐ x ☐
☐

3.
☐ x 2 x 3
6 x ☐
☐

4.
☐ x ☐ x 5
☐ x ☐
20

5.
☐ x 2 x 4
10 x ☐
☐

6.
3 x 5 x 2
☐ x ☐
☐

7.
☐ x ☐ x ☐ x ☐ x ☐ x ☐
9 x 9 ☐
81 x 9
☐

8.
3 x 3 x 2 x 2 x ☐
☐ x ☐ ☐
☐ x 4
☐

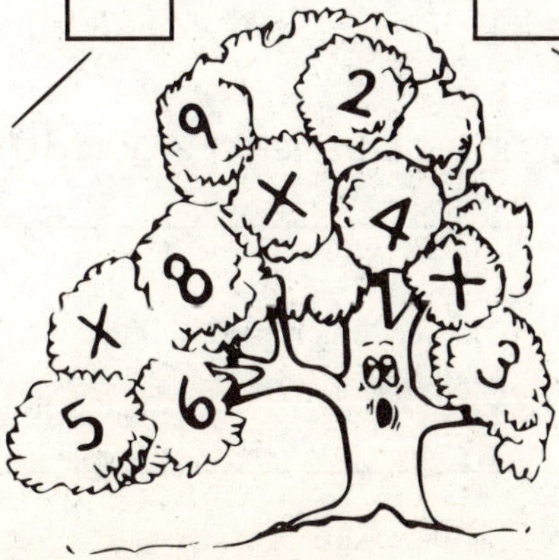

Name ______________________________ Date ______________

Positively Prime

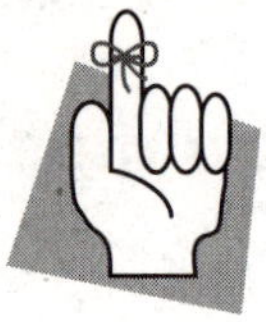

A **prime number's** only factors are 1 and itself.

Answer the questions.

1. Can an even number by prime? Explain.

____

2. Are all odd numbers prime? Explain.

____

3. Is the product of 2 prime numbers also prime? Explain.

____

4. Look at a multiplication table. What can you say about the numbers inside the table?

____

5. Consider the number 143.

a. Is 2 a factor? ______

b. Is 3, 6, or 9 a factor? ______

c. Is 4 or 8 a factor? ______

d. Is 5 or 10 a factor? ______

e. Is 7 a factor? ______

f. Do you think 143 is prime? ______

g. Try dividing 143 by prime numbers larger than 10. Can you find a factor? ______

h. Is 143 prime? ______

6. Find all the prime numbers between 2 and 100.

____

7. Explain your strategy for deciding whether or not a number is prime. Do you use any "tricks" to save time?

____

Name ______________________________ Date ______________

Number Changer

A number changer uses rules to make new numbers. Put a number IN and a different number comes OUT. Use the rules shown. Print the new numbers in OUT.

1. Rule: +3

IN	12	14	16	18	20	22
OUT						

2. Rule: +5

IN	170	172	174	176	178	180
OUT						

3. Rule: +4

IN	33	35	36	39	41	43
OUT						

4. Rule: +6

IN	151	153	155	157	159	161
OUT						

Name ______________________ Date ____________

Functions

Complete the table for each function rule given below.

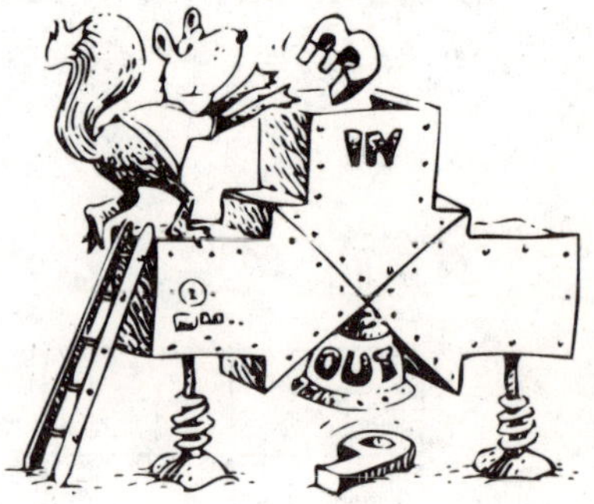

1. Rule: $m = n + 4$

IN(n)	12	14	16	18	20	22
OUT(m)	16	18	20			

2. Rule: $m = 3n$

IN(n)	0	1	2	3	4	5
OUT(m)						

3. Rule: $m = 3n - 3$

IN(n)	2	4	6	8	10	12
OUT(m)						

Find the function rule for each table below.

4.

IN(x)	6	7	9	11	14	16
OUT(y)	10	11	13	15	18	20

Rule: $y =$ ______

5.

IN(x)	1	3	6	8	10	13
OUT(y)	4	12	24	32	40	52

Rule: $y =$ ______

6.

IN(x)	10	13	16	19	22	25
OUT(y)	8	11	14	17	20	23

Rule: $y =$ ______

Name ______________________ Date ______________

What Do You Mean by Median?

The **mean** is the average found by adding all values and dividing by the number of values.

The **median** is the number that is exactly in the middle of the ordered data.

Example: Lenny loves basketball. He scored the following points per game.

Game	Points
1	5
2	10
3	3
4	14
5	3

median: 3, 3, (5) 10, 14
The median is 5 points per game.

mean: 5 + 10 + 3 + 14 + 3 = 35; 35 ÷ 5 = 7
The mean is an average of 7 points per game.

Study the data to correctly answer the questions.

Student	Number of Books Read
Anna	9
Carlos	5
Brian	7
Jada	8
Lin	11

1. What is the mean? ______________

2. What is the median? ______________

Tanya's scout troop made beaded animals to sell and raise funds for a camping trip.

Troop Members	Number of Bead Animals Made
Tanya	17
Cho	15
Maria	11
Avishai	14
Lucy	9
Kelly	6
Yong	21
Maya	6
Beth	9

3. What is the mean? ______________

4. What is the median? ______________

Name ______________________________ Date ______________

Growing Patterns

Draw the next shape in the pattern.

Fill in the table. Look for patterns.

Shape	1st	2nd	3rd	4th	5th	6th	7th	8th	9th	10th
Number of Triangles	2	4	6							

1. Describe the pattern for the number of triangles.

____

2. Explain how you can figure out the number of triangles if you know which shape it is.

____

3. How many triangles will be in the 15th shape? __________ the 20th? __________

4. Explain how you can figure out the number of triangles in the next shape if you know the number of triangles in the current shape.

____

5. If *S* represents the shape number, write an equation for finding the number of triangles, *T*.

T = __________ .

Name ______________________ Date ______________

Ship Shape

Study each set and draw points on the graph according to the coordinates given. The order of each coordinate is **(*x*, *y*)**. Then connect the dots in order to form geometric shapes. The first one is done for you.

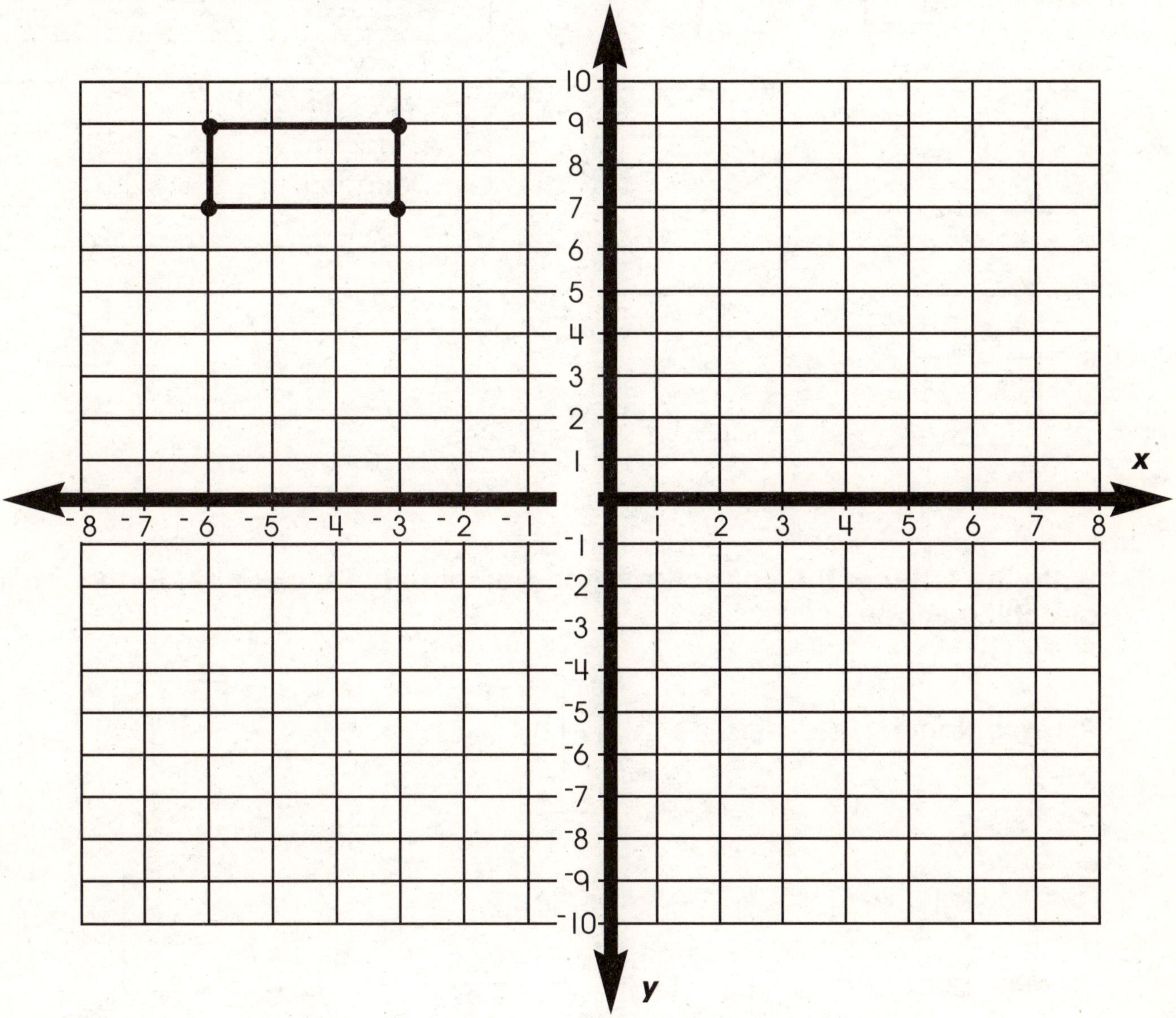

1. (-6, 7) (-6, 9) (-3, 7) (-3, 9)

2. (-7, -4) (-6, -2) (-4, -4) (-3, -2)

3. (-5, -5) (-3, -8) (-2, -5)

4. (2, 2) (2, 3) (7, 2) (7, 3)

5. (2, 5) (2, 7) (3, 4) (3, 8) (5, 4) (6, 5) (6, 7) (5, 8)

6. (3, -2) (3, -6) (5, -2) (5, -6)

7. (2, -9) (3, -7) (5, -7) (6, -9)

Name ______________________________ Date ______________

Classifying Polygons

Write the name of each polygon.

Polygon Name	Number of Sides
Triangle	3
Quadrilateral	4
Pentagon	5
Hexagon	6
Heptagon	7
Octagon	8
Decagon	10
Dodecagon	12

1. 

____

2. 

____

3. 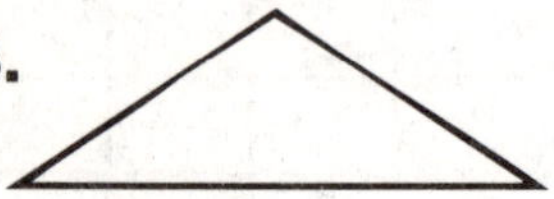

____

4. 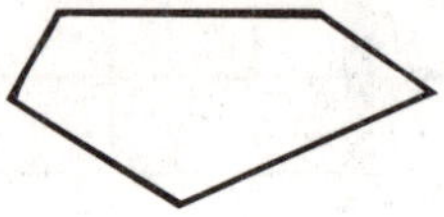

____

5. 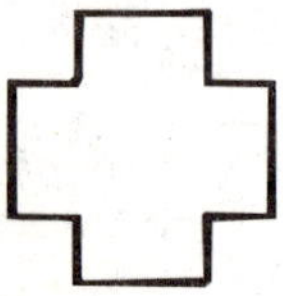

____

6. 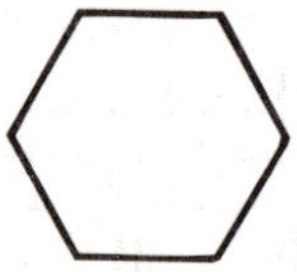

____

7. 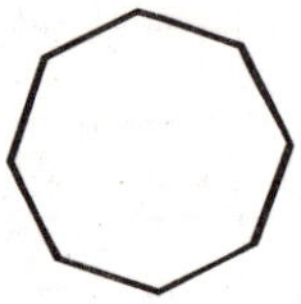

____

8. 

____

Write the letter of the correct polygon name on the blank next to the matching shape.

Polygon Name

a. triangle

b. quadrilateral

c. pentagon

d. hexagon

e. heptagon

f. octagon

_____ **9.** 

_____ **10.** 

_____ **11.** 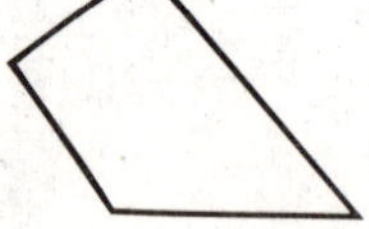

_____ **12.** 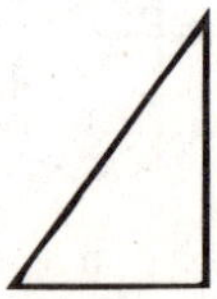

_____ **13.** 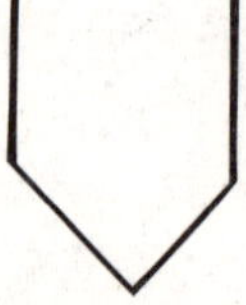

_____ **14.** 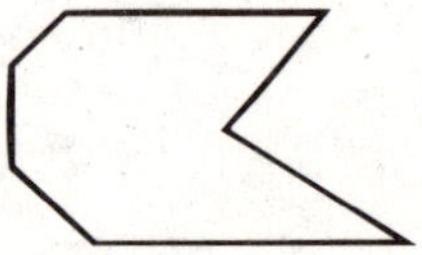

Name ____________________ Date ____________

Prisms and Pyramids

Many three-dimensional shapes fit into two categories: **prisms** and **pyramids**. Examples of prisms and pyramids are given below. The shaded portions of each shape are called **bases**. The other sides are called **faces**.

Prisms

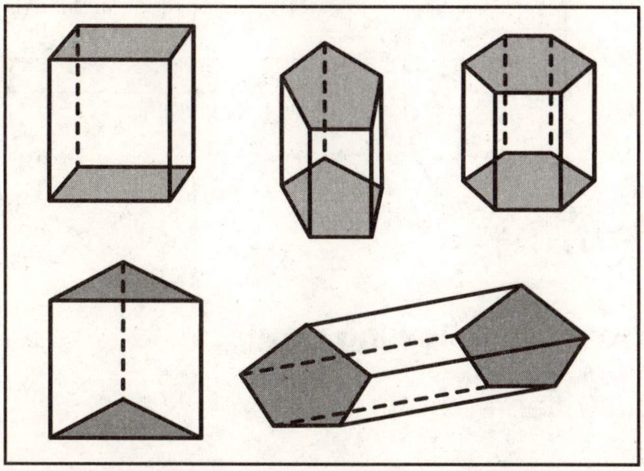

Pyramids

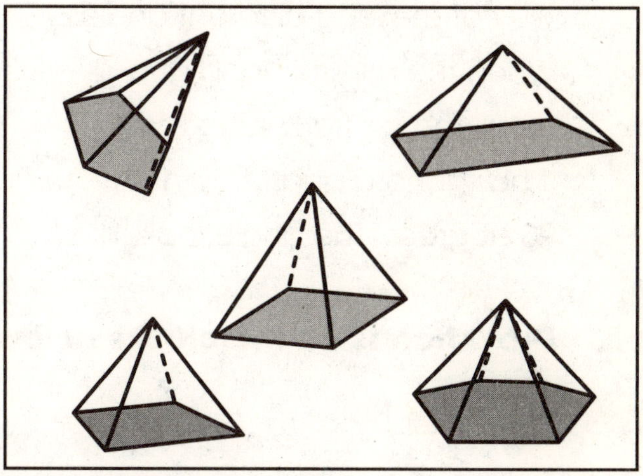

Use the prisms and pyramids above to answer the questions.

1. Examine the prisms and pyramids. Look for similarities and differences. Make a list of characteristics that define each category.

Prism Characteristics	Pyramid Characteristics
____________________	____________________
____________________	____________________
____________________	____________________
____________________	____________________

2. Modify each list. Make the list as short as possible, using only the necessary characteristics.

____________________	____________________
____________________	____________________

3. Explain how you chose the characteristics.

____

Name ______________________ Date ______________

Measuring Angles

The units for measuring angles are called **degrees**. One degree is one-ninetieth of a right angle. There are 360 degrees in a circle.

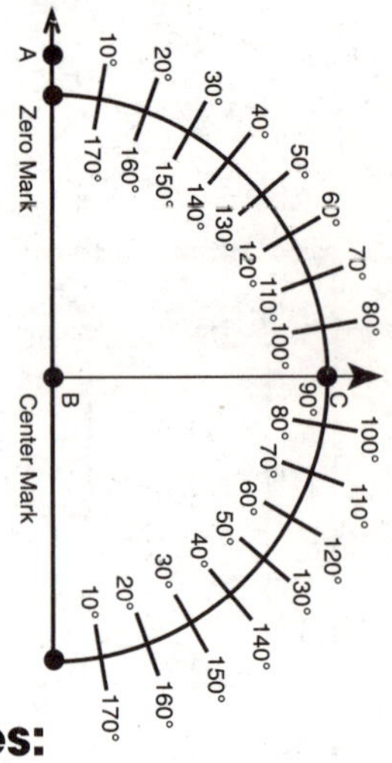

Using a clock face is a simple way of showing different angles. When the minute hand of a clock moves from 12 to 3, it has gone a quarter turn or 90 degrees. The angle looks like this:

Draw hands on the clocks below to show the following angles:

1. 180 degrees

2. 30 degrees

Measure the angle. How many degrees does the minute hand turn for each?

3. 12 o'clock to 5? ____________

4. 12 o'clock to 9? ____________

5. 12 o'clock to 7? ____________

6. 12 o'clock to 1? ____________

7. 12 o'clock to 4? ____________

8. 12 o'clock to 8? ____________

9. 12 o'clock to 10? ____________

10. 12 o'clock to 11? ____________

Name ______________________________ Date ______________

Puzzling Perimeters

Perimeter = the distance around a shape
P = side + side + side + side

Jason is helping to build a tennis court at a local park. Help him take measurements to buy materials.

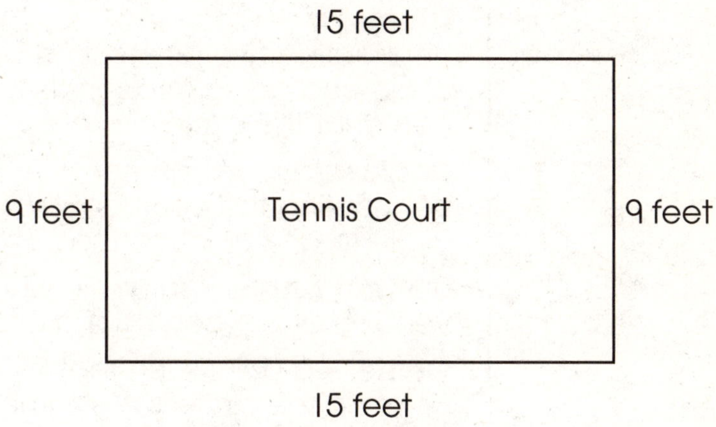

1. Using the perimeter formula, find the perimeter of the court.

____

2. Fencing is sold in sections of 3 feet. How many sections of fence will Jason need to buy to go around the entire court?

____

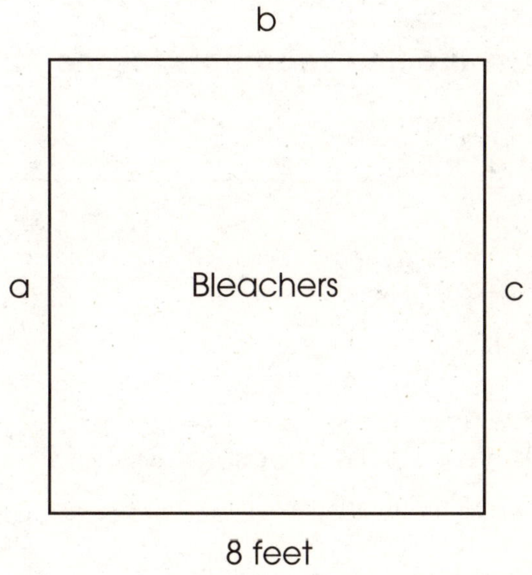

3. The park service decides to build a spectator area near the court. Jason wants it to be a perfect square. Can you find the perimeter?

____

4. How many sections of fencing will Jason need to buy to fit around the bleachers?

____

Name ______________________________ Date ______________

Exploring Circumference and Diameter

Study the definitions in the term box and look closely at the circle to understand and answer the questions below.

Terms

Circumference—the distance around a circle

Diameter—a segment connecting two points on a circle and going through the center of the circle

Radius—a line segment connecting the center of a circle to any point on the circle

Central Angle—an angle whose vertex is at the center of a circle

Center—a point such that every point on the circle is the same distance from it

Chord—any line segment that connects two points on a circle

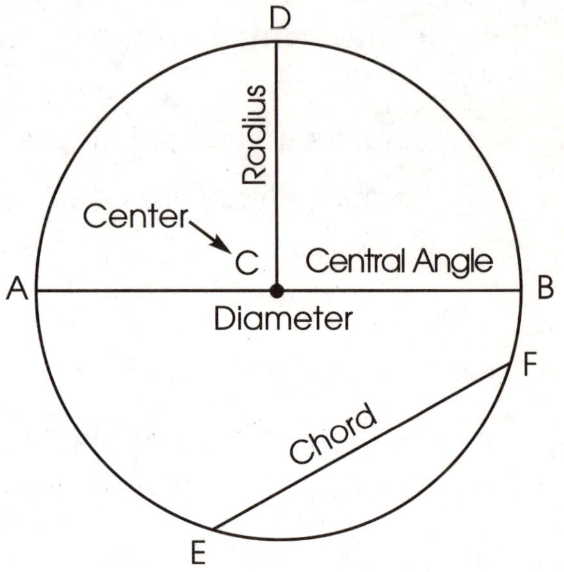

List the line segments for the following.

1. Radius ______________

2. Diameter ______________

3. Chord ______________

4. What is the measurement of the central angle? ______________

5. If the radius is 3.5 feet, what is the diameter? ______________

6. If the diameter is 4 feet and 12 inches, what is the radius?

____

7. If the radius is 9 yards, how many inches is the diameter?

____

8. If the diameter is 4 feet and 18 inches, how long is the radius?

____

0-7424-1945-2 — *Using the Standards*

Name ______________________ Date ______________

The Better Buy

Answer the questions below.

1. A bag of apples, containing 24 apples, costs $3.00. The same type of apple can be bought individually for $0.15 a piece. Which is the better buy? Explain.

____

2. Carpet cleaner comes in 2 sizes: 24 oz. for $3.08 or 36 oz. for $4.99. Which is the better buy? Explain.

____

3. Jamal is buying a group of solar power panels. He knows that a minimum of 3,456 square inches of panels are needed for generating the power he needs. The panels come in 2 sizes: 18 inches by 30 inches or 24 inches by 36 inches.

a. If he buys the smaller panels, how many will he need? Explain.

____

b. If he buys the larger panels, how many will he need? Explain.

____

c. The smaller panels cost $42.89 each, and the larger panels cost $86.40 each. Which size offers the better buy? Explain.

____

d. How much will the panels cost? Explain.

____

4. Explain how to find the better buy for 2 items of different sizes.

____

Name ______________________________ Date ______________

Calling All Units

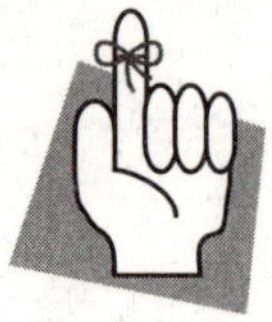

I cm = ——

I inch = ————

Use the lines above to answer the questions.

I. Compare the lengths of the lines above. About how many centimeters make up I inch? Describe the strategy you used to get your answer.

____

____

2. Mr. Hanson's fourth-grade class took the following measurements, but they forgot to write down the units. Some of the students measured in inches and some in centimeters. Help them figure out which measurements were taken in inches and which in centimeters.

Object	Measurement	Units
binder length	8.5	
binder width	28	
desktop width	60	
desktop length	18	
desk height	36	
door width	30	
door height	210	

3. Mr. Hanson says all measurements should be recorded in inches. There isn't time to take the measurements again. Use your answer from problem I to find each object's measurement in inches.

____

____

4. Describe the strategies you used to solve problems 2 and 3.

____

____

Name ______________________ Date ____________

Is That Enough?

For each problem, determine the various amounts that are needed and then answer the question.

1. The pattern for a Halloween costume calls for $3\frac{1}{4}$ yards of cloth that is 45 in. wide (114 cm). The clerk tells you she has sold almost all of her black material. She measures the bolt of cloth that remains. It is 45 in. wide. She has only 8 ft. (2.4 m) left.

Is that enough to make the costume? ______________________

2. You need a piece of carpet for a basement playroom. It needs to cover most of the floor, but it cannot be bigger than 244 cm (96 in.) long and 305 cm (120 in.) wide. You've measured your shoe and know that it is about 23 cm (9 in.) long. You measure a piece of carpet by stepping across it, toe to heel. It measures 10 of your steps in one direction and 13 in the other direction.

Is that enough carpet? ______________________

3. To have enough room at the Thanksgiving table, Mother had to add 3 leaves. When the table is this long, she needs to us a tablecloth that is 270 cm (106 in.) long. Betty found a pretty gold tablecloth that she wanted her mother to buy. The package says that the tablecloth is 3 m long.

Is the gold tablecloth large enough? ______________________

4. Tom wants a bookshelf that is big enough to hold all of his books. He lines up his books vertically and measures them. They stand in a row 216 cm (85 in.) long. The bookshelf he is planning to buy has 3 shelves that are each 76 cm (30 m) wide.

Is the bookshelf big enough? ______________________

Name ____________________ Date __________

Spinner Fun

Use the spinner for each problem to answer the questions.

1. Look at the spinner. What is the probability that the arrow will land on—

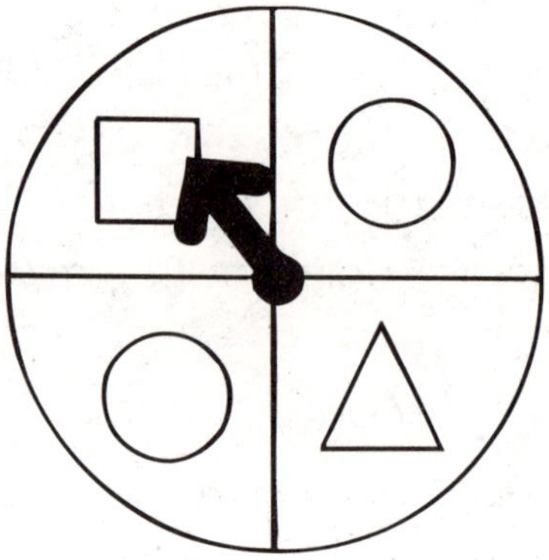

a. a circle? __________

b. a square? __________

c. a triangle? __________

d. Which shape has the greatest chance (probability) of having the arrow land on it? ____________________

e. Why do you think that? ____________________

____

2. Look at the spinner. What is the probability that the arrow will land on—

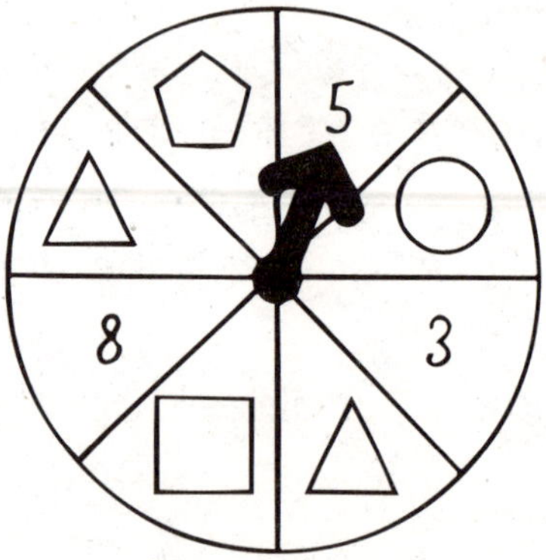

a. a shape? __________

b. a number? __________

c. a number or shape? __________

d. a circle? __________

e. a triangle? __________

f. a pentagon? __________

g. a square? __________

h. a 3? __________

i. an 8? __________

j. a 5? __________

k. a 5 or 8? __________

Name ______________________________ Date ______________

At the Library

A **frequency table** is a good way to show information. Frequency tables show **how often** something has occurred.

Answer the following questions using the frequency table below.

Books Checked Out by Students					
Type	**Monday**	**Tuesday**	**Wednesday**	**Thursday**	**Friday**
Nonfiction	23	20	26	18	12
Fairy Tales	11	14	8	15	7
Adventure	29	21	32	24	16
Mystery	32	20	26	36	30

1. How many nonfiction books were checked out during this week? ____________

2. How many fairy tales books were checked out during this week? ____________

3. How many adventure books were checked out during this week? ____________

4. How many mystery books were checked out during this week? ____________

5. What kind of book was checked out most often during this week? ____________

6. What kind of book was checked out least often during this week? ____________

Name ______________________________ Date ______________

Science Trip

The science class is planning a field trip to Chicago to visit the Museum of Science and Industry. There are 18 students in the class, and each student needs $40.00 to cover the expenses. The class decided to sell candy to raise money.

Answer the following questions using the chart below. Be sure to answer in complete sentences.

Weekly Class Sales				
	Week One	**Week Two**	**Week Three**	**Week Four**
Amount Raised	$282.00	$176.00	$202.00	$150.00

1. What is the weekly average of money raised based on 4 weeks of candy sales?

____

2. What is the average amount of dollars raised per child in 4 weeks of candy sales?

____

3. Has the class met its goal of $40.00 per child?

____

4. Did they raise more than enough money or not enough money?

____

5. How much above or beneath their goal per child did the class earn?

____

Name ______________________________ Date ______________

Finding Averages

Find the mean, median, mode, and range of each set of data below.

Mile Relay Practice Times	
Day	**Time (minutes)**
Monday	3.29
Tuesday	3.24
Wednesday	3.48
Thursday	3.24
Friday	3.89

1. mean ______________

median ______________

mode ______________

range ______________

Candy Bars Sold	
Day	**Number of Bars**
Monday	127
Tuesday	225
Wednesday	93
Thursday	82
Friday	111
Saturday	137
Sunday	82

2. mean ______________

median ______________

mode ______________

range ______________

Test Scores

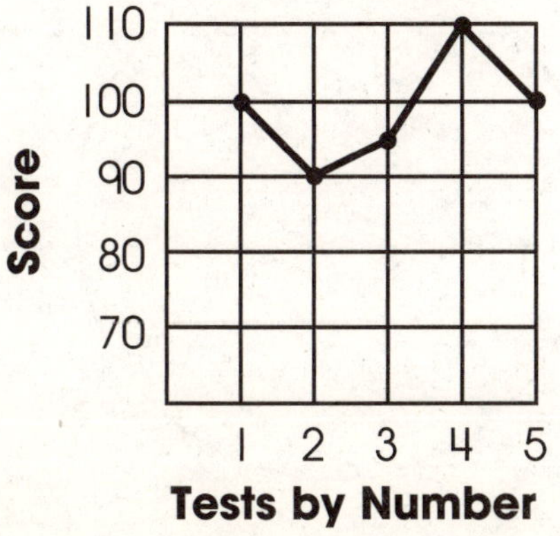

3. mean ______________

median ______________

mode ______________

range ______________

0-7424-1945-2 — *Using the Standards*

Name ______________________ Date ____________

Graph It

Use the following information to complete the circle graphs.

1. Birthplaces of the first 10 U.S. Presidents:

Virginia	60%
Massachusetts	20%
New York	10%
South Carolina	10%

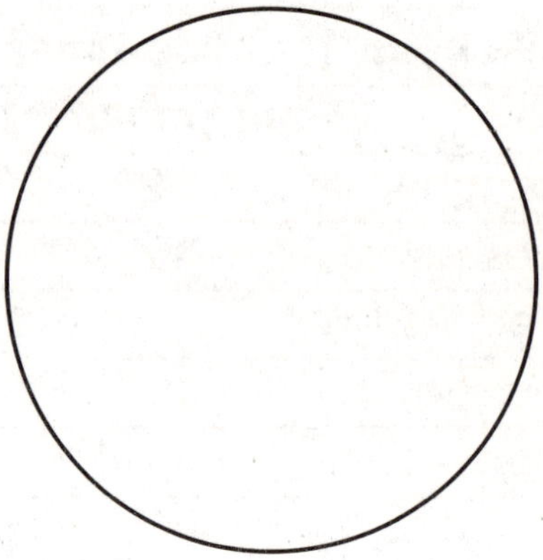

2. Trash collected on Earth Day:

paper	50%
aluminum cans	15%
plastic	15%
rubber	10%
glass	10%

3. Pizza preferences:

cheese	30%
cheese/pepperoni	20%
cheese/mushroom	10%
deluxe	40%

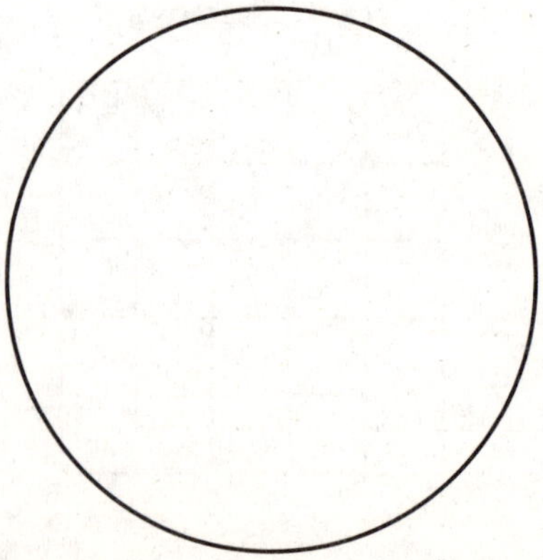

Standards in Science

Science means exploration, whether it involves classroom experiments or field trips. A standards-based science curriculum recognizes that a vital part of science education is active exploration and discovery. The National Science Teachers Association (**www.nsta.org**) has developed a series of resources called *Pathways to the Science Standards* to guide student learning in science. NSTA divides science knowledge into the following areas:

- Science as Inquiry
- Physical Science
- Life Science
- Earth and Space Science
- Science and Technology
- Science in Personal and Social Perspectives
- History and Nature of Science

At all levels of inquiry, students should work through the scientific process. Identify the hypothesis or concept to be tested; perform an experiment; collect data; interpret the results; summarize the findings.

Hot Tip

Space for Science. With a limited amount of resources available, how can you create the best possible science environment for your students? A sturdy plastic science cart can be a wonderful addition to your classroom. Fill the cart with tools for scientific inquiry—clipboards with paper for recording observations, thermometers, scales, microscope, containers, string, rulers, calculators, nature samples. After presenting a question to your class, allow them to select their own materials to test the hypothesis. This encourages active learning and saves space too!

An increased understanding of science as a process of exploration will lead students naturally to cross-curricular endeavors. Science is linked to math in recording and reporting data; to language arts in communicating the findings; to social studies in understanding the ways scientific discoveries change life for people and cultures.

Activity List

Most fifth graders love science experiments and are capable of inventing and testing them on their own. As a springboard for discovery, demonstrate a simple science experiment (see Activity 1). Then encourage your students to create some experiments of their own or try an experiment listed in a science text. Another great way to explore science is to have students investigate their surroundings outdoors (see Activity 2).

Activity 1–Making Carbon Dioxide

Standards: Science as inquiry, science in personal and social perspectives
Goal: Students will observe the build-up of carbon dioxide in a cup of yeast.
Materials: 2 tablespoons sugar, cup, water, yeast, plastic wrap
Activity:

1. Put 2 tablespoons of sugar in a cup of water and add a little yeast. Stir and cover tightly with plastic wrap.
2. Wait a day until bubbles have appeared.
3. Holding a lit candle over the top, remove the plastic wrap. The candle will go out because the glass is full of carbon dioxide made by the yeast feeding on the sugar.

Activity 2–Fungi Gardens

Standards: Science as inquiry, life science
Goal: Students will look for fungi samples outdoors and gather a sample for observation.
Materials: Students will need sealable plastic bags, craft sticks, and a magnifying lens.
Activity: Take a hike to a place where things are growing in the shade all day. Fungi can be found on tree trunks, on toadstools, or other shady places. Explain that fungi are not plants or animals. Fungi belongs in a group entirely of its own. Allow students time to look for fungi. When they find some, they should use the craft stick to remove some and place a sample in a sealable plastic bag. Students later add a piece of bread to the bag with their fungi and let it grow in a dark place. They study the results with a magnifying glass and report to the class. Sample discussion questions for this activity are given below.

1. Where did you find your fungi? What was it growing on or near?
2. Was the fungi growing in a cluster or clump?
3. How big was the fungi you found? Does it have an odor? What color is it?

Name ______________________ Date ____________

Sample Test

Read the passage. Then choose the correct answer for each question.

Ryan wanted to find out if people could tell the difference between the taste of cold tap water and cold bottled water. He filled one glass pitcher with tap water and another glass pitcher with bottled water. Then he placed the pitchers in the same refrigerator overnight.

1. Before completing his experiment, Ryan guessed that people would not be able to tell the difference between the two types of water. What part of the scientific process does this guess involve?
- **a.** listing the materials
- **b.** stating a hypothesis
- **c.** organizing data
- **d.** stating a conclusion

2. How should Ryan complete his experiment?
- **a.** He should ask several people to taste the tap water.
- **b.** He should ask several people to taste the bottled water.
- **c.** He should ask several people to taste both types of water and guess which is tap water and which is bottled water.
- **d.** He should ask several people to taste both types of water and tell which one they like best.

Read each item. Then choose the correct answer.

3. According to the food pyramid, which of the following food categories should you eat the most from?
- **a.** oils, fats, and sweets
- **b.** breads, cereals, rice, and pasta
- **c.** milk, yogurt, and cheese
- **d.** meat, fish, poultry, and eggs

4. Which body parts are included in the respiratory system?
- **a.** spinal cord, medulla, brain stem
- **b.** heart, arteries, veins
- **c.** lung, bronchial tube, trachea
- **d.** stomach, liver, pancreas

GO

Name ______________________ Date ____________

Sample Test (cont.)

Use the table to answer the questions.

Time Required for Pendulum to Complete Ten Swings

Pendulum	**Time of Ten Swings (in seconds)**			
	1st Trial	**2nd Trial**	**3rd Trial**	**Average**
30-cm string with large paperclip	9	8	10	9
30-cm string with small paperclip	8	9	10	9
15-cm string with large paperclip	6	7	6	6.3
15-cm string with small paperclip	5	6	7	6

5. Why is it important to have more than 1 trial in an experiment?

____

6. Which swings faster, a pendulum with a long string, or a pendulum with a short string?

____

7. Which swings faster, a pendulum with a large paperclip, or a pendulum with a small paperclip?

____

8. Write a conclusion for this experiment based on the data in the table. What additional steps could you take to prove your conclusion?

____

____

STOP

0-7424-1945-2 — *Using the Standards*

Name ______________________________ Date ______________

Tools of the Trade

The most basic part of science involves asking questions. Why do leaves come off the trees in the fall? Why does toothpaste contain fluoride? Is it possible for people to travel to the planet Mars? Being a good scientist means knowing what tools you need to help you answer a question (or **hypothesis**).

Look at the questions below. Match each question to the tool(s) you might use to help you answer it. Write the letter on the blank.

_____ **1.** Does a Thermos really keep things colder than a regular cup?

_____ **2.** How do I find the Big Dipper in the sky?

_____ **3.** Is anything living in the pond near my house? The water looks clear.

_____ **4.** How many cars cross the street in front of our school each day between 3 P.M. and 4 P.M.?

_____ **5.** Which has more inside—a pint of milk or a liter of soda?

_____ **6.** Whose apple is heavier—mine or my best friend's?

_____ **7.** What kinds of insects are in the dirt at our park?

_____ **8.** What do you use to heat a solution of water and salt?

_____ **9.** Just how tall is my backpack, anyway?

_____ **10.** What birds live near my house?

a. hand lens

b. yardstick

c. binoculars

d. thermometer

e. telescope

f. microscope

g. graduated cylinder

h. tally chart

i. balance scale

j. beaker, Bunsen burner

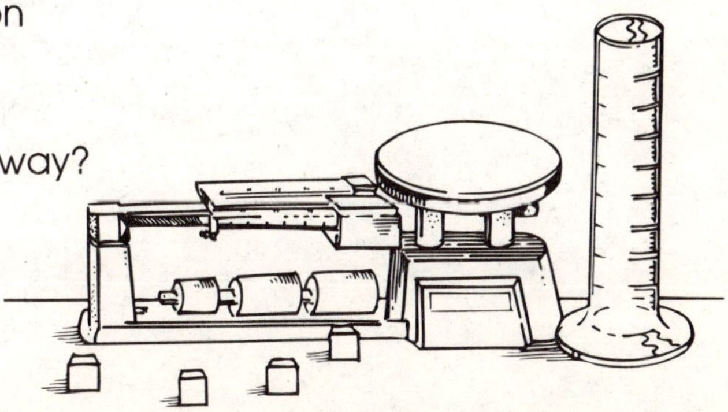

Name ______________________________ Date ______________

Lights, Colors, and Prisms

Purpose: Understand that rays of sunlight are actually made up of different colors. Break sunlight into the individual colors using a prism.

Materials: prisms of different sizes and shapes, sunlight (strong), white paper, crayons or colored pencils

Introduction: Have you ever seen a rainbow after a storm? As the rays of sunlight pass through the raindrops in the atmosphere, the light is bent and reflects off the drops, resulting in the seven colors known as the spectrum. In this activity, you will experiment with prisms and determine the order for the colors in the spectrum.

Procedure:

1. Select three different types of prisms. Draw and describe each one in the table on page 101.
2. Allow bright sunlight to shine through your prism and project a spectrum on the floor or wall.
3. While one member of your group holds the prism, the remaining members should observe the rainbow that is produced. Record which color is the top color on the spectrum and the order of the other colors.
4. Repeat steps 2 and 3 for the other two prisms.

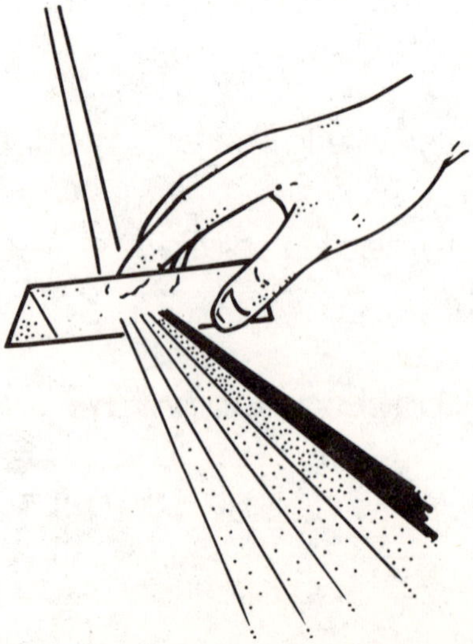

Name ______________________________ Date ______________

Lights, Colors, and Prisms (cont.)

Use the directions on page 100 to fill in the table.

	Prism #1	Prism #2	Prism #3
Shape of the prism (sketch)			
First color in the spectrum			
Order of the remaining colors			

Post-Lab Questions

1. What happens when light shines through a prism?

____

____

2. What did you notice about the order of the colors shown in the rainbow?

____

____

0-7424-1945-2 — *Using the Standards*

Name ______________________________ Date ______________

How Does a Frog Catch Its Lunch?

Purpose: Describe how a frog, toad, or lizard uses its tongue to capture insects. Understand that animals have adaptations that assist them in survival.

Materials: party blower, 3-cm strip of Velcro, 30-cm piece of string or ribbon, pencil, graph paper

Introduction: Frogs are found throughout the world. They live in ponds, lakes, marshes, and other wetland areas. To capture insects, a frog uses its long sticky tongue. The frog flips its tongue over and out and then draws it back into its mouth after capturing its prey. This is an example of an adaptation that aids the frog in its survival.

Procedure:

1. Unroll the party blower so that the end is in your hand.
2. Attach the "rough" piece of Velcro to the party blower by folding it over the end. (This is the frog's "tongue.")
3. Make a loop with the string.
4. Attach the "soft" piece of Velcro to the loop by folding it over the end of the loop. This secures the Velcro on both sides of the string. (This is the "fly.")
5. Working with a partner, take turns pretending to be a "frog" and try to catch the "fly" as your partner slowly dangles the string in front of the party blower.
6. Predict how many flies you will be able to catch in 30 seconds and in 1 minute. Record your estimate in the table on page 103.
7. Have your partner count how many times you try to catch the fly in 30 seconds and how many flies are caught. Do the same for your tries in 1 minute. Record your observations in the table.

Name ______________________ Date ______________

How Does a Frog Catch Its Lunch? (cont.)

Use the directions on page 102 to fill in the table.

Time	Estimated number of flies caught	Total tries	Total caught
30 seconds			
1 minute			

Post-Lab Questions

1. How close was your estimate of how many flies you would catch?

____

2. Describe how you felt trying to catch "flies" with your pretend frog tongue.

____

3. Did you catch any more flies on your second try? Why do you think that might be?

____

4. Explain why a frog's tongue is a special adaptation that helps it to survive.

____

____

____

____

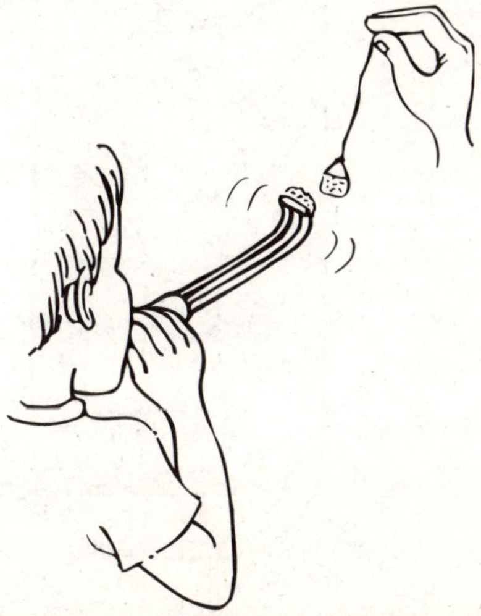

0-7424-1945-2 — *Using the Standards*

Name ______________________________ Date ______________

Water on the Run

Purpose: Determine how texture and particle size affect soil permeability.

Materials: two empty 2-liter plastic soft-drink bottles with caps containing several holes, scissors, tape, aquarium gravel or very coarse sand, marble chips or large pieces of gravel, clay, graduated cylinder, spoon, watch with a second hand, water, 250-ml beaker

Procedure:

1. Convert your soft-drink bottle to a funnel by cutting it in half with scissors. Place the cap filled with holes on the mouth of the bottle. Invert the top half of the bottle, mouth downward, into the bottom half (see Figure 1).

2. Use a beaker to measure 200 ml of clay.

3. Transfer the clay from the beaker into the funnel. Measure 200 ml of water and pour it on top of the clay in the funnel (see Figure 2).

Figure 1

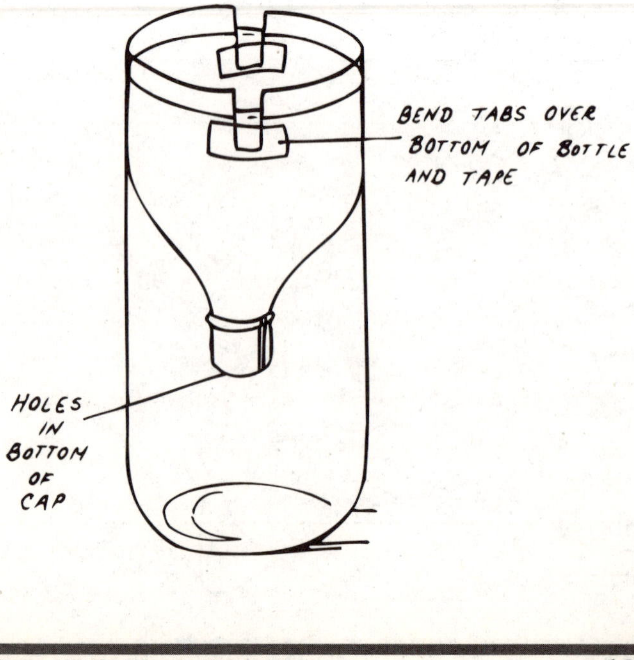

Figure 2

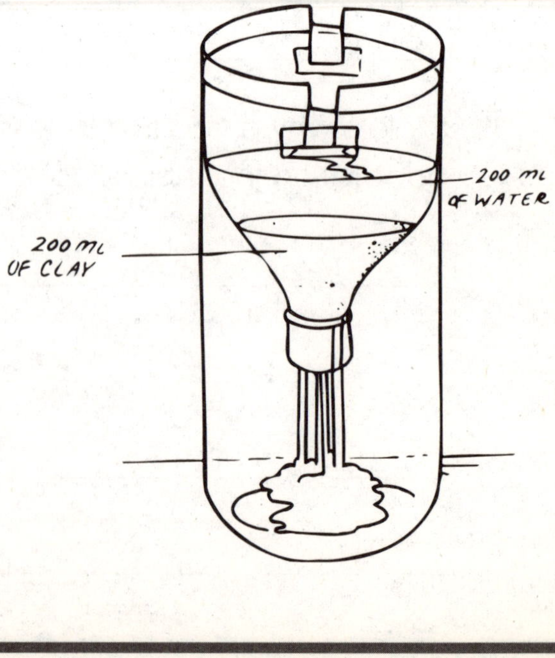

Name ______________________________ Date ______________

Water on the Run (cont.)

4. Time how long it takes for the water to drain through the clay, until it is level with the top of the clay. Record this time in the table below.

5. Remove the clay from the funnel and wash the funnel and cap. Repeat steps 2 through 4 using 200 ml of aquarium gravel to represent your medium-sized particles. Record your results in the table.

6. Remove the aquarium gravel and wash the funnel and cap. Repeat steps 2 through 4 using 200 ml of marble chips to represent large particles. Record your results in the table.

Time Required for Water to Seep into Soil

	Clay Particles (small)	**Aquarium Gravel** (medium)	**Marble Chips** (large)
Time required			

Post-Lab Questions

1. Through which particles did water pass the most quickly? the most slowly?

____

2. Would you expect rain to form puddles in sand, silt, or clay? Why?

____

3. Which would be least likely to erode quickly—sand, silt, or clay particles?

____

Name ______________________________ Date ______________

Humanity vs. Technology

Think about the differences in the ways humans and computers perform tasks. Although computers can greatly simplify our daily lives, some things are still done best by humans. Consider why that is true as you complete this page.

Here are 8 descriptions of how tasks might be performed. Some best describe computers. Place a C in those blanks. For items that best describe humans, place an H in the blanks.

_____ **1.** It works consistently with very large amounts of information.

_____ **2.** It can adapt new information to the present situation.

_____ **3.** It performs the same task in slightly different ways each time.

_____ **4.** It can recall every piece of information it has ever received.

_____ **5.** Partway through a task, it can change its mind and proceed another way.

_____ **6.** It can perform many different tasks at the same time.

_____ **7.** It can select when it wants to work on which task.

_____ **8.** It needs a small amount of space to store a lot of information.

Now write additional descriptions. Write one that fits computers and one that tells about humans.

Computers
9. ____

Humans
10. ____

Name ______________________________ Date ______________

Bacteria Hunt

Purpose: Predict places bacteria might live. Take a sample of bacteria from different locations and grow a bacteria culture.

Materials: nutrient-rich agar, petri dishes, cotton swabs, distilled water, grease pencil, resealable plastic bags

Procedure:

1. Moisten (not soak) a cotton swab in distilled water.
2. Decide where to take a sample of bacteria by running the cotton swab over the object. For example, swab the mountpiece of the water fountain or the inside of a wastebasket.
3. Without touching the swab to any other object, transfer the bacteria sample onto the nutrient-rich agar by rolling the swab across the agar.
4. Using a grease pencil, write the name of the location from which the sample was taken on the lid of a petri dish. Include the date.
5. Place the lid on the petri dish and carefully seal it inside the plastic bag.
6. Check the agar dish every few days and record your observations about what is growing in the table below.

Date/Time	Observations

Post-Lab Questions

1. Where did you collect your bacteria sample?

____

2. How can you help prevent the spread of bacteria?

____

Name ______________________ Date ____________

Who Were They?

To be a scientist means to be a person who challenges accepted ideas. Throughout history, discoveries in science changed the ways that people thought and lived. Use an encyclopedia or other reference tool to find out about the famous scientists below. How might the world be different today without the discoveries of each person?

Albert Einstein

When did he live? ______________________

What did he do? ______________________

Galileo Galilei

When did he live? ______________________

What did he do? ______________________

Marie Curie

When did she live? ______________________

What did she do? ______________________

Sir Isaac Newton

When did he live? ______________________

What did he do? ______________________

Jane Goodall

When did she live? ______________________

What did she do? ______________________

Standards in Social Studies

Social studies encourages students to be full and active participants in the world around them through an ever-increasing understanding of their community, state, country, and world. The National Council for the Social Studies (NCSS) standards can be found at: **www.socialstudies.org/standards**. The NCSS lists ten thematic strands:

- Culture
- Time, Continuity, and Change
- People, Places, and Environment
- Individual Development and Identity
- Individuals, Groups, and Institutions
- Power, Authority, and Governance
- Production, Distribution, and Consumption
- Science, Technology, and Society
- Global Connections
- Civic Ideals and Practices

Use the broad spectrum of knowledge covered by social studies to develop your own thematic cross-curricular units. Social studies exploration naturally lends itself to other subjects: reading more about a people or place, using math to interpret data, drawing on scientific principles to understand climate and environment, and tapping into language arts skills to report what has been discovered.

Hot Tip

Theme-Based Learning in Social Studies. Take full advantage of the cross-curricular possibilities of social studies by creating richly textured theme-based units for your students. Students working through a unit on the Amazon might do all of the following in different subject areas:

- read books and stories about the rain forest
- learn new vocabulary as they study the layers of the rain forest
- interpret data about animals or people by reading graphs and charts
- discover the location of the Amazon by looking at maps
- examine the main exports and make a graph to communicate this data
- use scientific evidence to understand the climate of the region
- become involved citizens as they learn about conservation efforts

Thematic units provide a dynamic way to connect learning across the curriculum areas and to deepen student connections to the world around them.

Activity List

Social studies engages students with the world around them. This can be as broad as their planet or as specific as their hometown. By the time students have reached fifth grade, it is a good time to strengthen their knowledge of United States history. Encourage students to explore the Presidents (see Activity 1) and the geography of this land (see Activity 2).

Activity 1–Presidential Experts

Standards: People, places, and environment; individuals, groups, and institutions; power, authority, and government
Goal: Each student will become an expert on a particular President by researching their President and creating a report to present to the class.
Materials: Students will need a blank notebook, research sources, as well as materials to create a bulletin board display.
Activity: Assign each student in your class a President. Depending on the size of your class, you may wish to assign more than one President to a student. Explain to students that they will become the experts on this President. They will fill their notebooks with information about the President they are researching. Allow time for library research as well as independent study. When students have had adequate time to fill their notebooks, they should create two things—a summary report and materials for a bulletin board display. They will present their President to the class. In this way, the class gets to know many Presidents at one time. You can include faces of the Presidents to add to a butcher-paper timeline as you learn about each one.

Activity 2–State Experts

Standards: People, places, and environment
Goal: Each student will become an expert on a particular state by researching their state and creating a report to present to the class.
Materials: Students will need a folder to collect brochures, research sources, as well as materials to create a bulletin board display.
Activity: Each student chooses (or is assigned) a different state. Students send away for brochures, maps, and other information for their state. (This is a good time to practice those business letter writing skills!) Students collect information in a folder, along with research from other sources. Students present their findings to the class in the form of a report or bulletin board display. You might also wish to decorate a map of the U.S. with information for each state, along with the state capitals.

Name ______________________ Date ____________

Sample Test

Read the paragraph and look at the pictograph. Use them to answer the questions.

As the Industrial Revolution spread throughout the United States, more and more people from other countries immigrated, or moved, to the United States. In the mid-1800s, many of the immigrants settled in the West and became farmers. But by the late 1800s, most new immigrants were settling in cities and seeking work in factories and mines.

The pictograph shows how many people immigrated to the United States from 1820 to 1920. Each  stands for 1,000,000 immigrants.

Number of People Who Immigrated to the U.S.	
1820 - 1840	
1841 - 1860	
1861 - 1880	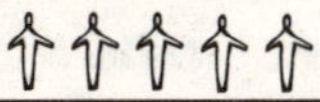
1881 - 1900	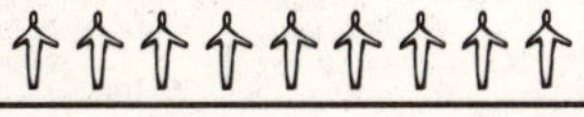
1901 - 1920	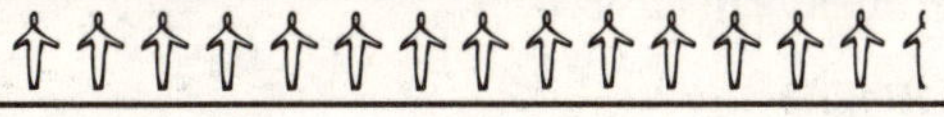

1. During which years did the greatest number of people immigrate?

____

2. Based on the information above, which of the following dates is closest to the start of the Industrial Revolution?
   a. 1820
   b. 1841
   c. 1861
   d. 1881

3. Why do you think most new immigrants of the late 1800s and early 1900s chose to live in urban areas instead of rural areas?

____

____

GO

Name ______________________ Date ______________

Sample Test (cont.)

Use the chart to answer the questions.

Price per Slice	Number Sold
$0.50	50
$0.75	40
$0.90	30

4. As the price of a slice of pizza goes up, what happens to the demand?
a. It goes up.
b. It goes down.
c. It goes up then down.
d. It stays the same.

5. Which price above brings the greatest amount of revenue?
a. $0.50
b. $0.75
c. $0.90
d. none of the above

Read each item. Choose the correct answer to each question.

6. Which of the following is not a country in Europe?
a. France
b. Italy
c. Ireland
d. Honduras

7. Who was President of the Union during the Civil War?
a. Thomas Jefferson
b. Abraham Lincoln
c. Franklin D. Roosevelt
d. Ulysses S. Grant

8. What were three reasons the American colonists had for starting the Revolutionary War?

____

____

____

____

STOP

Name ______________________________ Date ______________

Amazing Americans

Some historical events influence the way we live and think today. In the box are names and dates of some Americans who led the way for changes to occur. Not all answers will be used.

a. *Brown v. Board of Education*	**b.** 1908	**c.** Amelia Earhart
d. Madeleine Albright	**e.** Neil Armstrong	**f.** Frances Perkins
g. Jane Addams	**h.** Sally Ride	**i.** Charles A. Lindbergh
j. Woodrow Wilson	**k.** Charles Wilkes	**l.** Maggie L. Walker
m. 1865	**n.** Robert Peary	**o.** 1920

Match the correct name or date to each description below. Write the letter in the blanks. There are more answers than questions, so cross out each item as you use it.

_____ **1.** first woman to serve as U.S. Secretary of State

_____ **2.** year of the first Model T car

_____ **3.** first person to fly solo across the Atlantic Ocean

_____ **4.** first person to walk on the moon

_____ **5.** first person to claim Antarctica as a continent

_____ **6.** year the Thirteenth Amendment was ratified, abolishing slavery

_____ **7.** year the Nineteenth Amendment was ratified, giving women the right to vote

_____ **8.** first woman in the U.S. to found a bank and serve as bank president; also was the daughter of a former slave

_____ **9.** first person to reach the geographic North Pole on the ice cap

_____ **10.** determined "separate but equal" schools were unconstitutional

When you are finished, use an encyclopedia or other reference tool to research the names in the box you did not use. Use the back of this page to write a question to match each name.

0-7424-1945-2 — *Using the Standards*

Name ______________________ Date ____________

Early Colonial Regions

The soil in the New England Colonies was filled with rocks and was not very fertile. There were dense forests and the climate was wet and cold. The colonists living here worked at fishing along the coastline, lumbering, and shipbuilding.

The Southern Colonies were different from the New England Colonies. The climate was mild and warm. The land was level and fertile, which made it excellent for growing tobacco, rice, and cotton.

The Middle Colonies had many coastal seaports and forestlands were plentiful. There were also excellent farmlands for growing wheat, rye, barley, corn, and fruits.

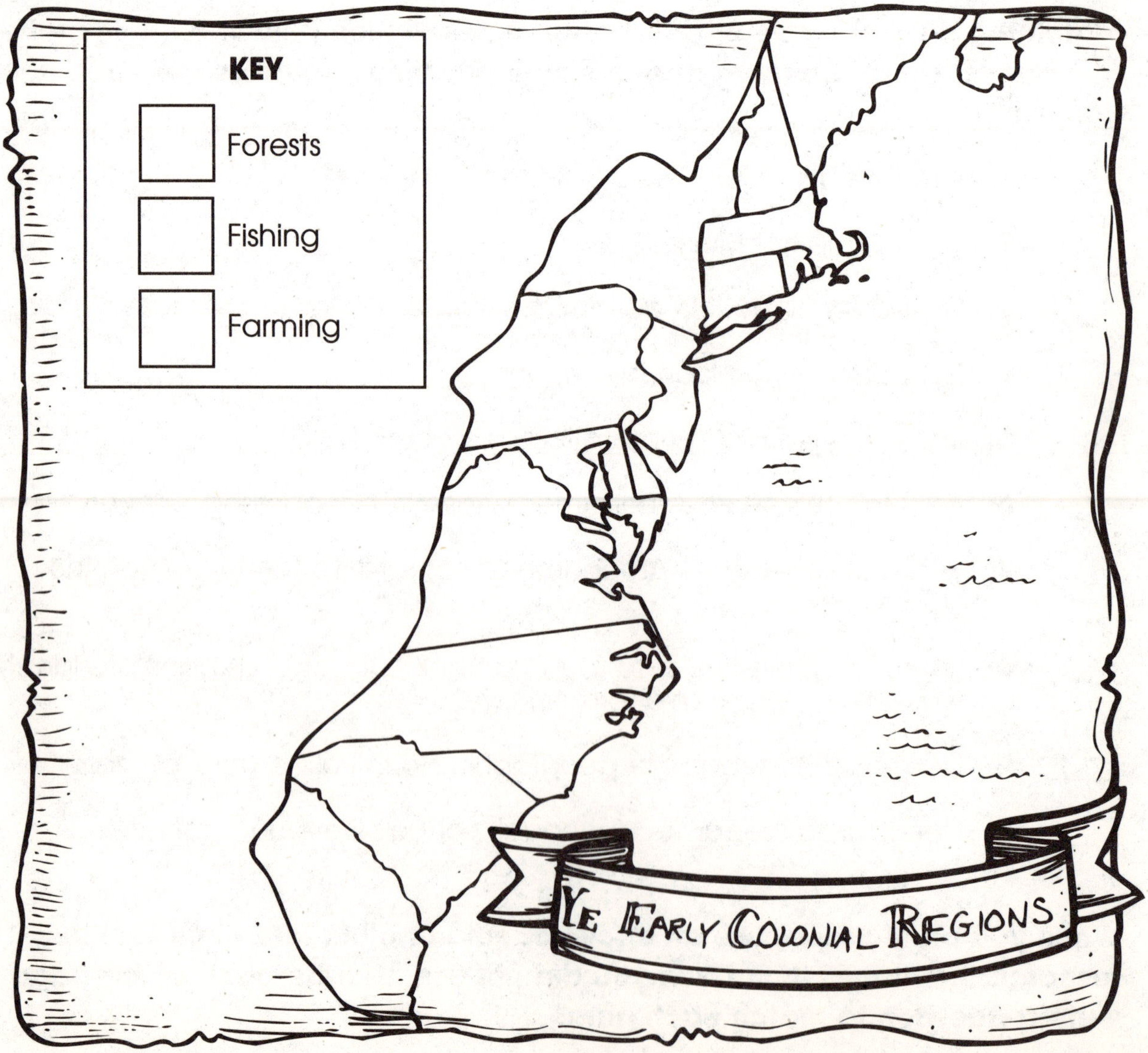

Name ______________________________ Date ______________

Early Colonial Regions (cont.)

Refer to page 114 to answer the questions.

1. Identify the following on the map on page 114. Use an encyclopedia or other reference tool to help you.

- Massachusetts
- Virginia
- Connecticut
- Rhode Island
- New Jersey
- New Hampshire
- New York
- Maryland
- Delaware
- Pennsylvania
- North Carolina
- Georgia
- South Carolina
- Atlantic Ocean

2. Shade the New England Colonies pink, the Middle Colonies yellow, the Southern Colonies green, the rest of the land tan, and the water blue.

3. Create a symbol for forests, fishing, and farming. Add it to the key on page 114. Then add each symbol to the map on the appropriate regions.

4. Which region has the most colonies? Why do you think this is so?

____

____

5. How did the climate affect the way the colonists lived in each region?

____

____

6. Which region would you want to live in?

____

Name ______________________________ Date ______________

In My Bag

Have you ever moved from one place to another? What did you pack? How did you move your things from one place to another? You might have put your things in boxes or suitcases and loaded them onto a moving truck. Early settlers in America moved in a very different way.

The earliest colonists came from England by ship. They made their homes right where they landed, on the eastern coast. As the colonies grew, travel was on horseback. Later, as the westward movement continued, settlers traveled by covered wagon.

Travel back in time to imagine what it might be like to move at different times in American history. Use an encyclopedia or other reference tool to help you learn more about transportation during each time. Then use what you have read to answer the questions below each story.

As your family sits by the fire one night, your father tells about the colonies across the ocean. It will mean leaving everything you know behind. What will it be like in that new world? You won't have room to bring much with you, only a small bag. What will you pack? What will it be like to travel on one of the sailing ships you have seen in the harbor? How do you feel about this news?

From	Year	Type of Transportation
England to America	1620	sailing ship

How I feel about moving ______________________________

____

What's in my bag ______________________________

____

What it might be like on the sailing ship ______________________________

____

Name ______________________ Date ____________

In My Bag (cont.)

You have never lived anywhere but Boston. Your family has a small house and you love your friends. You know there are other colonists living in other places, but it doesn't interest you much. Until you hear that you will be moving to Rhode Island. Your family will travel by horseback. You will have room for a small satchel.

From	Year	Type of Transportation
Boston, Massachusetts to Providence, Rhode Island	1700	horseback

How I feel about moving ______________________

____

What's in my satchel ______________________

____

What it might be like on the horse as I travel ______________________

____

Ever since you were little, you have loved the mountains. Sometimes you wondered what was on the other side. Now you have a chance to find out! Your family is moving to the western territory. Some of your cooking supplies will be packed in the wagon, along with your clothes and food. You have a small bag to pack.

From	Year	Type of Transportation
North Carolina to Louisiana Territory	1800	covered wagon

How I feel about moving ______________________

____

What's in my bag ______________________

____

What it might be like in the wagon as I travel ______________________

____

Name ______________________ Date ____________

Give Me the Picture

Agricultural Products of Brazil

Key

☐ rubber	☐ bananas
☐ cattle	☐ rice
☐ sheep	☐ forest products
☐ manioc	☐ coffee
☐ cacao beans	☐ sugar cane

Name ______________________________ Date ______________

Give Me the Picture (cont.)

Design a symbol for each product listed in the table below. Then illustrate the map on page 118 to show where these agricultural crops are produced.

Product	**Symbol**	**Directions**
rubber		W of Pôrto Velho N of Pôrto Velho
bananas		NE of Teresina W of Salvador
cattle		W of Pôrto Alegre S of Cuiabá island NW of Belém S of Brasília
rice		N of Teresina W of Pôrto Alegre W of Brasília
sheep		W of Pôrto Alegre SW of Recife E of Teresina
forest products		E of Manaus
manioc		W of Salvador S of Teresina
coffee		NW of São Paulo NE of Rio de Janeiro
cacao beans		S of Salvador
sugar cane		N of São Paulo S of Recife

Name ______________________________ Date ______________

Demand Worksheet

Assume you have $20 to spend on CDs. Answer each question and then plot the information on the graph below.

1. How many CDs could you buy if the price of each was $4? ______________
2. How many CDs could you buy if the price of each was $5? ______________
3. How many CDs could you buy if the price of each was $10? ______________
4. How many CDs could you buy if the price of each was $20? ______________
5. What do you notice about demand as the price increases? ______________

____

____

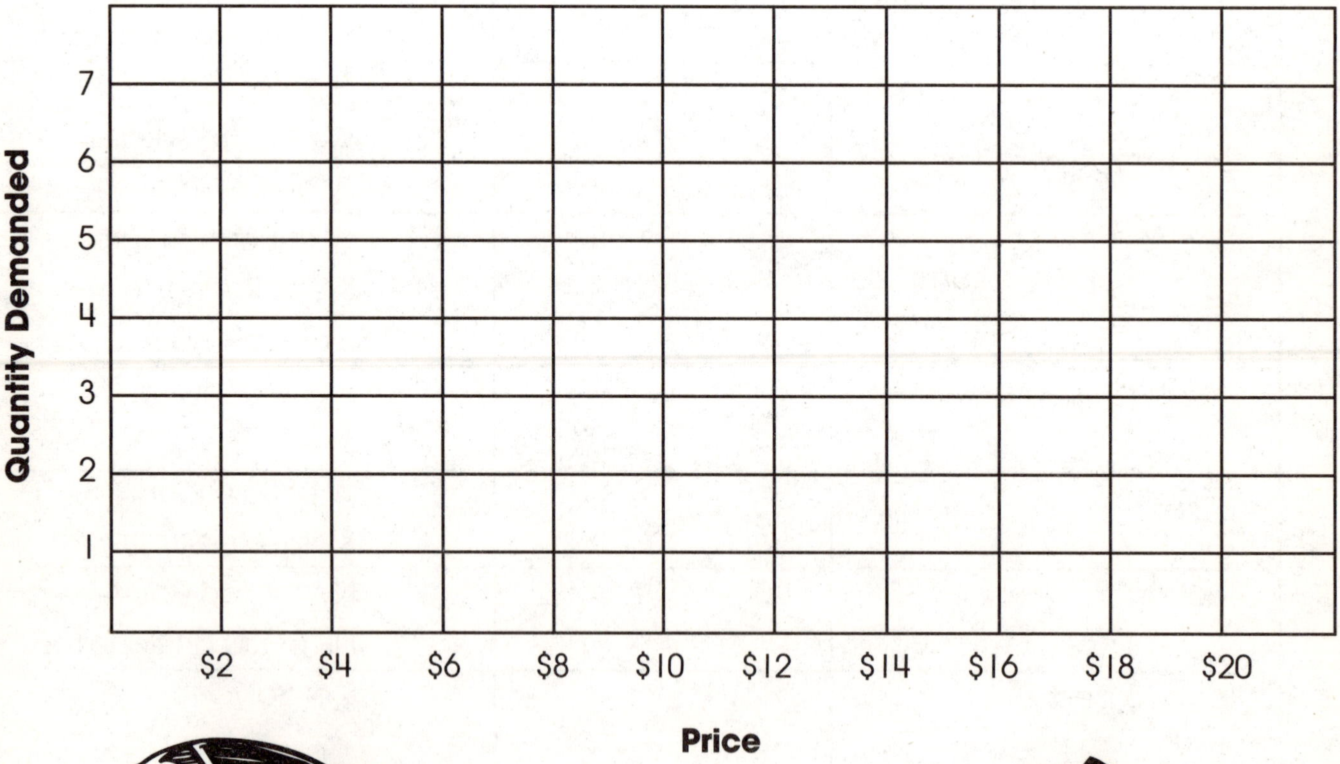

Name ______________________ Date ____________

Space History

Listed below are 15 important events in the history of space travel. Can you place them in the proper order? In the blank at the end of each item, write the year the event took place. In the left-hand blank, number the events from 1–15. Use an encyclopedia or other reference tool to help you find the answers.

____ **1.** first "space walk" by Alexei Leonov ________

____ **2.** *Viking 1* and *Viking 2*, from the U.S.A., make controlled landings on Mars ________

____ **3.** launch of the Hubble Space Telescope ________

____ **4.** Armstrong and Aldrin, in the *Apollo 11*, land on the moon ________

____ **5.** launch of the first American satellite, *Explorer 1* ________

____ **6.** first launch of America's Space Shuttle ________

____ **7.** first liquid-fuel rocket launched by Goddard, U.S.A. ________

____ **8.** first close-up pictures of Mercury by *Mariner 10*, U.S.A. ________

____ **9.** First successful unmanned probes to the moon: *Luna 1*, *Luna 2*, *Luna 3*, former Soviet Union ________

____ **10.** first manned flight around the moon, *Apollo 8*, U.S.A. ________

____ **11.** disaster with America's shuttle *Challenger* ________

____ **12.** V.2 rockets developed by Wernher von Braun and his German team first flown ________

____ **13.** launch of *Skylab*, America's first space station ________

____ **14.** *Voyager 2* flew past Neptune ________

Name ______________________ Date ______________

Branches of Government

The powers of the national government are distributed among the legislative, executive, and judicial branches. Use reference resources to identify the power of each of the three branches. List the powers below inside the appropriate box.

Legislative Branch	Executive Branch	Judicial Branch

- impeach the President
- nominate members of the federal judiciary
- pass laws over the President's veto by two-thirds majority vote of both Houses
- establish committees to oversee activities of the executive branch
- overrule decisions made by lower courts
- disapprove appointments made by the President
- declare laws made by Congress to be unconstitutional
- veto laws passed by Congress
- declare actions of the executive branch to be unconstitutional
- propose amendments to the U.S. Constitution

Reading

Sample Test....................17-20

1. a **2.** d **3.** a **4.** d
5. a **6.** a **7.** b **8.** c
9. b **10.** d **11.** b **12.** d
13. a **14.** d **15.** c **16.** a
17. Spring. There are small buds on the trees and a gentle breeze.
18. Steven
19. He doesn't know whether or not to skip school with his friend Jared.
20. He will go to school. He knows it is wrong and seeing the school in the distance helps him decide.

Word Play 21

1. H **2.** A **3.** H **4.** S
5. A **6.** S **7.** H **8.** S
Answers may vary for 9–12.
9. dirty, tidy
10. take apart, join
11. serious, funny
12. greedy, giving
Correct story homophones: fair, pair, hares, breaks, fur, won, sale, hares, stake, too, brakes, Pete, Terry.

America's Beauties 22

1. e **2.** g **3.** i **4.** a
5. b **6.** j **7.** f **8.** c
9. d **10.** k **11.** h **12.** l

Two Boys, Two Cultures.......23

1. false **2.** false **3.** true
4. true **5.** false **6.** true
7. false **8.** false **9.** false
10. false

Paradise...............................25

Answers will vary.

Ancient Farming 27

1. It was the only way they could get food.
2. The ashes from the burn fertilized the soil.
3. The mud from the bottom of the lake was very fertile and rich.
4. Terraces helped reduce erosion.
5. Answers will vary.

Write Now 28

1. science fiction
2. poetry
3. historical fiction
4. biography
5. folktale
6. fairy tale
7. science fiction
8. biography
9. fantasy
10. poetry

I Plant..................................29

1. The poet plants a tree to celebrate beauty and remind her of a grandparent who has died.
2. The poet remembers the loving embrace of her grandparent.
3. The poet is celebrating the beauty around her.
4. anchored
5. life, celebrate

Matchmaker 30

1. e **2.** b **3.** c
4. d **5.** a

A Polaroid Moment 31

1. a
2. running underneath the swing after pushing it
3. She has a big smile on her face.
4. Answers will vary. Some possibilities include happiness, enjoyment, pleasure.
5. So they can all remember the fun of that moment.
6. Answers will vary. One possibility is "The Underdog."

King Tut's Tomb 33

1. O **2.** O **3.** F **4.** O
5. F **6.** O **7.** F **8.** F
9. F **10.** O

Welcome to Our Assembly 34

1. g **2.** a **3.** d **4.** c
5. h **6.** b **7.** e **8.** f

Have I Got a Job for You.......................35

Tad—5
Blanche—3, 4
Anselm—2, 3
Zoe—1
Perry—3

The Right Cause 36-37

Captain Colossal: b, d, i
my sister: f, k, l
Ben: c, e, j
tornado: a, g, h

Theme 38

1. theme **2.** moral **3.** theme
4. moral **5.** moral **6.** theme
7. Answers will vary.

Language Arts

Sample Test....................42-45

1. b **2.** a **3.** c **4.** a
5. d **6.** a **7.** d **8.** d
9. a **10.** c **11.** d **12.** b
13. d **14.** c **15.** b **16.** d
17. d **18.** d **19.** a **20.** b
21. a **22.** c **23.** d **24.** c

Pen Pals 47

Li Lui
house: apartment building
city: Beijing
country: China
TV show: cartoons*
food: shrimp chips
drink: soda

uniform: blue warm-up suit
favorite subject: art, Chinese
least favorite subject: math

Yena
house: one-floor house
city: Accra
country: Ghana
TV show: cartoons*
food: plantains
drink: fruit juice
uniform: brown dress, yellow shirt
favorite subject: science
least favorite subject: French

Audience and Purpose 48

1. Shoppers: Shoppers are inconvenienced because they must park several blocks away. Parking a distance from stores where they shop forces them to carry packages a long way.
2. City police: Drivers are parking illegally and blocking entranceways. They are parking too close to alleyways and are jeopardizing safety of pedestrians. Consequently, city policemen are spending too much time writing tickets and seeing that vehicles are towed from restricted parking places.
3. Store owners: Merchants are losing business because people cannot find parking places. Shoppers prefer the mall to the downtown area because of parking convenience.
4. Pedestrians: Crossing the street has been difficult and even dangerous for shoppers because their view is obstructed by vans, SUVs, and other large vehicles.

Sentence Combining 51

Answers may vary.

1. Dennis enjoys his creative writing class because it gives him an opportunity to try writing different types of stories.
2. Writers can solve some of the problems they face through group discussions.
3. Mandy enjoys writing poetry, but does not enjoy writing mystery stories.
4. Proofreaders read for errors only after they first edit content.
5. The bases were loaded, but Mighty Casey struck out.

Identifying Sentences 52

1. sentence	**2.** fragment
3. sentence	**4.** sentence
5. fragment	**6.** sentence

7–8. fragments: A very old city. Because running with the bulls can be dangerous. Rewritten sentences will vary.

Compound Subjects and Predicates 53

1. Humans and mice can solve mazes.
2. Mice and humans like to eat cheese.
3. Humans are able to reason and speak. (or) Humans are able to reason and are able to speak.
4. Mice eat and sleep in their nests.
5. Humans and mice care for their babies.
6. Mice wake up and look for food at night. (or) Mice wake up at night and look for food.

Editing Skills 55

Autumn is a nice time of year in **M**ichigan. **S**ome people like to go water-skiing in the summer. Most people enjoy the changes autumn brings. New sounds, sights, and smells arrive with the crisp wind that replaces the soft summer air**.**

Early in the season, many people like **to** pick **a**pples and make good apple pies. **This** is the time of year for enjoying apple cider, donuts, and hayrides. Pumpkin pies make delicious desserts on **T**hanksgiving Day. What is your favorite season**?** Mine**'**s definitely autumn!

As the temperatures outside drop, so do the pretty leaves on the trees. Families work together raking **them** into piles. Children can be heard laughing as **they** jump into big piles of leaves. Later, the smell of burning leaves often fills the autumn air.

As the autumn air grows even cooler, tree branches begin **to** look bare under a gray sky. November winds soon whisk away the fallen dried leaves. Michigan says farewell **to** gentle autumn and hello **to** the harsh winter that lies ahead.

Spelling Practice 56

1. c	**2.** b	**3.** a	**4.** a
5. b	**6.** d	**7.** a	**8.** a

Math

Sample Test....................61–64

1. c	**2.** d	**3.** d	**4.** a
5. d	**6.** b	**7.** c	**8.** a
9. c	**10.** c	**11.** e	**12.** e
13. b	**14.** d	**15.** d	**16.** b
17. d	**18.** d	**19.** c	**20.** d
21. b	**22.** c	**23.** d	**24.** a
25. d	**26.** b	**27.** c	**28.** d
29. b	**30.** a	**31.** d	**32.** a

Place Value 65

1. 562,174 **2.** 200,518,736
3. 65,270,948,301 **4.** b **5.** a
6. c **7.** f **8.** d **9.** e
10. 711.009, 711.9, 711.95, 712.001, 712.01, 712.09, 712.10

Number Crunching 66

1. 300,000 + 2, three hundred thousand, two
2. 10,000 + 900 + 200 + 5, nineteen thousand, two hundred five
3. 30,000,000, + 1,000,000 + 400,000 + 20,000 + 5,000 + 600 + 20, thirty-one million, four hundred twenty-five thousand, six hundred twenty
4. 50,000,000 + 7,000,000 + 900,000 + 6,000 + 600 + 8, fifty-seven million, nine hundred six thousand, six hundred eight
5. 30,000,000 + 1,000,000 + 400,000 + 6,000 + 400 + 10 + 5, thirty-one million, four hundred six thousand, four hundred fifteen

What Number Am I? 67

1. 42 **2.** 15 **3.** 83
4. 26 **5.** 75

Lines of Integers 68

1. $^{-}2$ **2.** 1 **3.** $^{-}4$ **4.** $^{-}2$
5. 1 **6.** 3 **7.** $^{-}9$ **8.** 2

How Long Would it Take? ...69

1. 126 friends (not including you)
2. 8:00 Tuesday morning
3. 8.3 minutes
4. 2 hours, 15 minutes

Which Is More? 70

1. a. 12 boxes of 24 chocolate bars
b. 15 x 18 = 270, 12 x 24 = 288

2. a. 16 bags of 25 buttons
b. 12 x 30 = 360, 16 x 25 = 400
3. c. the room that is 12 x 14 ft.
d. 12 x 14 = 168, 15 x 11 = 165
4. multiplication

Cycling for Fractions 71

1. $\frac{3}{4}$ **2.** $\frac{1}{4}$ **3.** $\frac{2}{4}$
4. $\frac{4}{12}$ **5.** $\frac{8}{12}$ **6.** $\frac{2}{12}$
7. $\frac{10}{12}$ **8.** $\frac{6}{12}$ **9.** $\frac{38}{36}$
10. $\frac{11}{36}$ **11.** $\frac{17}{36}$ **12.** $\frac{5}{26}$

Freaky Fractions 72

1. $\frac{2}{3} = \frac{1}{3} + \frac{1}{3} \approx 0.33 + 0.33 \approx 0.66$

2.
$\frac{2}{5} = \frac{1}{5} + \frac{1}{5} = 0.2 + 0.2 = 0.4$
$\frac{3}{5} = \frac{2}{5} + \frac{1}{5} = 0.4 + 0.2 = 0.6$
$\frac{4}{5} = \frac{3}{5} + \frac{1}{5} = 0.6 + 0.2 = 0.8$

3. $\frac{2}{6} = \frac{1}{6} + \frac{1}{6} \approx 0.17 + 0.17 \approx$ 0.34 (similar for other fractions)

4. a. $\frac{2}{3} > \frac{3}{5}$
b. $\frac{2}{5} > \frac{1}{3}$
c. $\frac{3}{4} < \frac{4}{5}$
d. $\frac{3}{5} > \frac{1}{2}$
5. Answers may vary. Students could compare the decimal equivalencies found in problems 1–3, find common denominators, or draw pictures.

Two-Stepping 73

1. $2.35
2. $3.45
3. $2.00
4. 8,904
5. $0.06
6. hamburgers—232

School Supplies 74

1. actual cost—$2.48
2. actual cost—$5.24
3. actual cost—$5.68
4. actual cost—$2.27
5. actual cost—$4.31
6. actual cost—$2.28

Factor Trees 75

Numbers are given only for the empty boxes for each problem.
1. 9, 18
2. 15, 3, 45
3. 3, 3, 18
4. 2, 2, 4, 5
5. 5, 4, 40
6. 15, 2, 30
7. 3, 3, 3, 3, 3, 3, 9, 729
8. 2, 9, 4, 4, 36, 144

Positively Prime 76

1. 2 is the only even prime number. All other even numbers have a factor of 2.
2. Every prime number, except 2, is odd. But, not all odd numbers are prime. 9 is odd and has a factor of 3.
3. No. The product will automatically have 2 additional factors besides itself and 1.
4. The multiplication table shows many numbers that are not prime. If a number is found on the table (so long as it is not in the "1 x" row or column), then it is not prime.
5. a–e. no
f. Answers may vary.
g. 143 ÷ 11 = 13
h. no
6. 2, 3, 5, 7, 11, 13, 17, 19, 23, 29, 31, 41, 43, 47, 53, 59, 61, 67, 71, 73, 79, 83, and 97
7. Answers may vary. Students could use a 100-chart and cross out all multiples of the numbers 2–10. They could then test the remaining numbers to see if any have prime factors.

Answer Key

Number Changer.................77

1. 15, 17, 19, 21, 23, 25
2. 175, 177, 179, 181, 183, 185
3. 37, 39, 40, 43, 45, 47
4. 157, 159, 161, 163, 165, 167

Functions..............................78

1. 16, 18, 20, 22, 24, 26
2. 0, 3, 6, 9, 12, 15
3. 3, 9, 15, 21, 27, 33
4. $y = x + 4$
5. $y = 4x$
6. $y = x - 2$

What Do You Mean by Median? 79

1. mean = $(9 + 5 + 7 + 8 + 11) \div 5 = 8$
2. 8
3. mean = $(17 + 15 + 11 + 14 + 9 + 6 + 21 + 6 + 9) \div 9 = 12$
4. 11

Growing Patterns.................80

Number of triangles: 2, 4, 6, 8, 10, 12, 14, 16, 18, 20

1. The number of triangles increases by 2 each time.
2. The number of triangles is 2 times greater than the shape number.
3. 30, 40
4. You can divide the number of triangles by 2, add 1, and then multiply by 2.
5. $T = 2 \times S$

Ship Shape..........................81

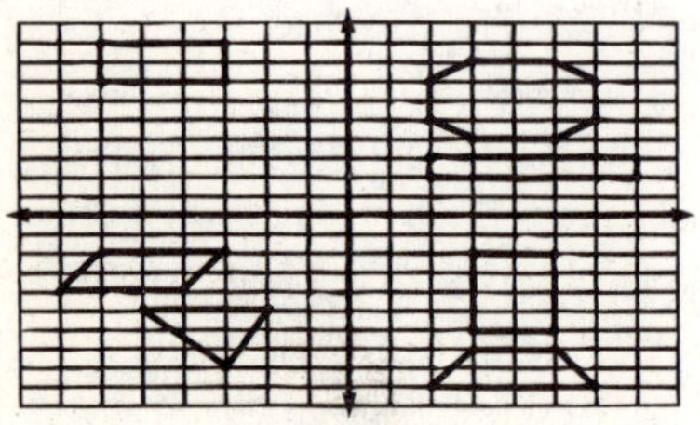

Classifying Polygons 82

1. pentagon **2.** decagon
3. triangle **4.** pentagon
5. dodecagon **6.** hexagon
7. octagon
8. quadrilateral (parallelogram)
9. d **10.** f **11.** b **12.** a
13. c **14.** e

Prisms and Pyramids...........83

1. Answers may vary.
2. Prisms have 2 parallel and congruent polygon bases connected by rectangular faces. Pyramids have 1 polygon base with triangular faces meeting at a vertex (or peak).
3. Answers may vary.

Measuring Angles................84

1.  **2.** 

3. 150° **4.** 270° **5.** 210°
6. 30° **7.** 120° **8.** 240°
9. 300° **10.** 330°

Puzzling Perimeters..............85

1. 48 feet
2. 16 sections
3. 32 feet
4. 11 sections

Exploring Circumference and Diameter 86

1. $\overline{CD}$
2. $\overline{AB}$
3. $\overline{EF}$
4. 90°
5. 7 feet
6. 2 feet 6 inches
7. 648 inches
8. 2 feet 9 inches

The Better Buy......................87

1. The bag of apples is a better buy. Each apple costs $3.00 ÷ 24 = $0.125, which is less than the single price of $0.15 per apple.
2. The 24 oz. size is the better buy ($0.128 per oz. vs. $0.139 per oz.).
3. **a.** 7 panels will be needed (18 x 30 = 540 sq. in.; 3,456 ÷ 540 = 6.4).
b. 4 panels will be needed (24 x 36 = 864 sq. in.; 3,456 ÷ 864 = 4).
c. The smaller panels are the better buy. Small panels cost $0.08 per square inch ($42.89 ÷ 540). Large panels cost $0.10 per square inch ($86.40 ÷ 864).
d. 7 small panels will cost $300.23 ($42.89 x 7).
4. Divide the price of each item by its size to find the price per unit. Then compare unit prices.

Calling All Units...................88

1. 1 inch is approximately 2.5 cm.
2. binder length 8.5 in.
binder width 28 cm
desktop width 60 cm
desktop length 18 in.
desk height 36 in.
door width 30 in.
door height 210 cm
3. binder width = 28 cm ÷ 2.5 = 11.2 in.
desktop width = 60 cm ÷ 2.5 = 24 in.

door height = 210 cm ÷ 2.5 = 84 in.
4. Answers may vary.

Is That Enough? 89

1. no
2. no
3. yes
4. yes

Answer Key

Spinner Fun 90

1. a. 2 in 4
b. 1 in 4
c. 1 in 4
d. circle
e. There are 2 circles.

2. a. 5 in 8
b. 3 in 8
c. 8 in 8
d. 1 in 8
e. 2 in 8
f. 1 in 8
g. 1 in 8
h. 1 in 8
i. 1 in 8
j. 1 in 8
k. 2 in 8

At the Library 91

1. 99 nonfiction books
2. 55 fairy tale books
3. 122 adventure books
4. 144 mystery books
5. mystery books
6. fairy tale books

Science Trip 92

1. $202.50
2. $11.25
3. no
4. not enough money
5. $28.75 beneath the goal

Finding Averages 93

1. mean: 3.43
median: 3.29
mode: 3.24
range: 0.65

2. mean: 122.43
median: 111
mode: 82
range: 143

3. mean: 99
median: 100
mode: 100
range: 20

Graph It 94

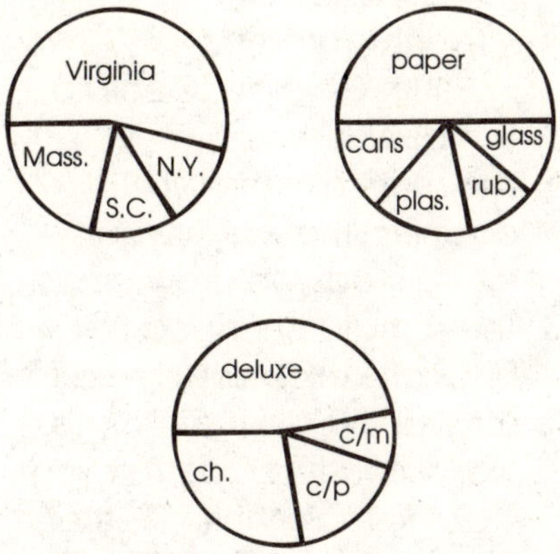

Science

Sample Test....................97–98

1. b **2.** c
3. b **4.** c
5. It is important to have more than 1 trial to get an accurate sampling of data.
6. A pendulum with a short string swings faster.
7. Paperclip size does not appear to affect the speed of the pendulum.
8. The length of a pendulum affects its rate of swing.

Tools of the Trade 99

1. d **2.** e
3. f **4.** h
5. g **6.** i
7. a **8.** j
9. b **10.** c

Lights, Colors, and Prisms 101

1. The prism breaks the light into individual colors.
2. red, orange, yellow, green, blue, indigo, violet

How Does a Frog Catch Its Lunch? 103

1–3. Answers will vary.
4. The frog's long tongue helps it grab insects as they fly by.

Water on the Run..............105

1. sand or marble chips, clay
2. Rain would form puddles in clay. Clay soil is not very water permeable.
3. clay

Humanity vs. Technology...................106

1. C **2.** H **3.** H **4.** C
5. H **6.** C **7.** H **8.** C
9–10. Answers will vary.

Bacteria Hunt.....................107

Answers will vary. Students should recognize the importance of washing hands and cleaning to prevent the spread of bacteria.

Who Were They?...............108

Albert Einstein—1879–1955; famous for his theory of relativity ($E = mc^2$).

Galileo Galilei—1564–1642; astronomer and physicist; built a telescope and studied the skies; motion of the pendulum.

Marie Curie—1867–1934; discovery of radioactivity leading to scientific breakthroughs in medicine such as the X-ray.

Sir Isaac Newton—1643–1727; astronomy, physics, mathematics; reflecting telescope, calculus, theory of universal gravitation.

Jane Goodall—born 1934; studies chimpanzees in east Africa; laid foundation for primate studies.

Social Studies

Sample Test...............111–112

1. 1901–1920
2. d

3. Most immigrants of the late 1800s and early 1900s might have chosen to live in cities rather than rural areas because of the increased opportunities available at new factories.

4. b **5.** b **6.** d **7.** b

8. Answers will vary. Some possibilities are: The British imposed unfair taxes on the colonists. The colonists were not allowed representation in the British government. Britain required the colonists to provide food, housing, and supplies to British soldiers. Colonists were killed by British soldiers during the Boston Massacre.

Amazing Americans........................113

1. d **2.** b **3.** i **4.** e
5. k **6.** m **7.** o **8.** l
9. n **10.** a

Early Colonial Regions..............115

1.

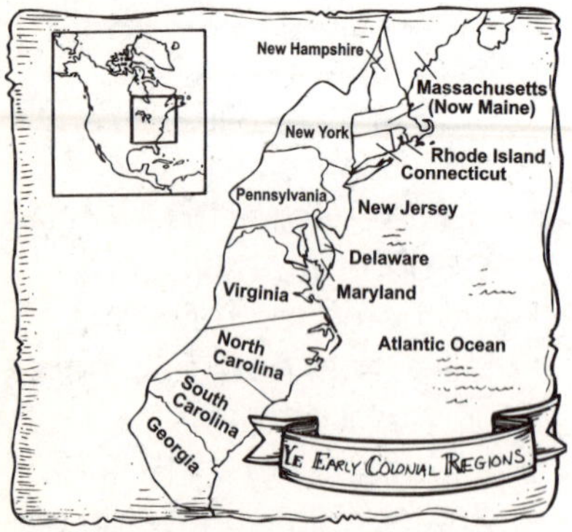

2. New England (pink): Massachusetts, Connecticut, New Hampshire, Rhode Island
Middle Colonies (yellow): New York, Pennsylvania, New Jersey, Delaware
Southern Colonies (green): Maryland, Virginia, North Carolina, South Carolina, Georgia

3. Symbols will vary.

4. The south has the most colonies. The warm weather made it easy to grow crops.

5. The climate changed the kinds of work colonists did for survival. Where the climate was suited to crops, farming was the main work. Where the climate was suited to fishing, colonists worked at that or lumbering and ship building.

6. Answers will vary.

In My Bag..................116–117

Answers will vary, but should reflect an appropriate understanding of each time period.

Give Me the Picture...............................118

Symbols will vary. One possibility given.

rubber = Ru
bananas = B
cattle = Ct
rice = Ri
sheep = Sh
forest products = FP
manioc = M
coffee = Co
cacao beans = CB
sugar cane = SC

Demand Worksheet.........................120

1. 5 **2.** 4
3. 2 **4.** 1

5. As price increases, demand goes down.

Space History 121

1. 5, 1965 **2.** 10, 1976
3. 14, 1990 **4.** 7, 1969
5. 3, 1958 **6.** 11, 1981
7. 1, 1926 **8.** 9, 1974
9. 4, 1959 **10.** 6, 1968
11. 12, 1986 **12.** 2, 1942
13. 8, 1973 **14.** 13, 1989

Branches of Government..................122

Legislative Branch
- impeach the President
- pass laws over the President's veto by two-thirds majority vote of both Houses
- establish committees to oversee activities of executive branch
- disapprove appointments made by the President
- propose amendments to the U.S. Constitution

Executive Branch
- nominate members of the federal judiciary
- veto laws passed by Congress

Judicial Branch
- overrule decisions made by lower courts
- declare laws made by Congress to be unconstitutional
- declare actions of the executive branch unconstitutional